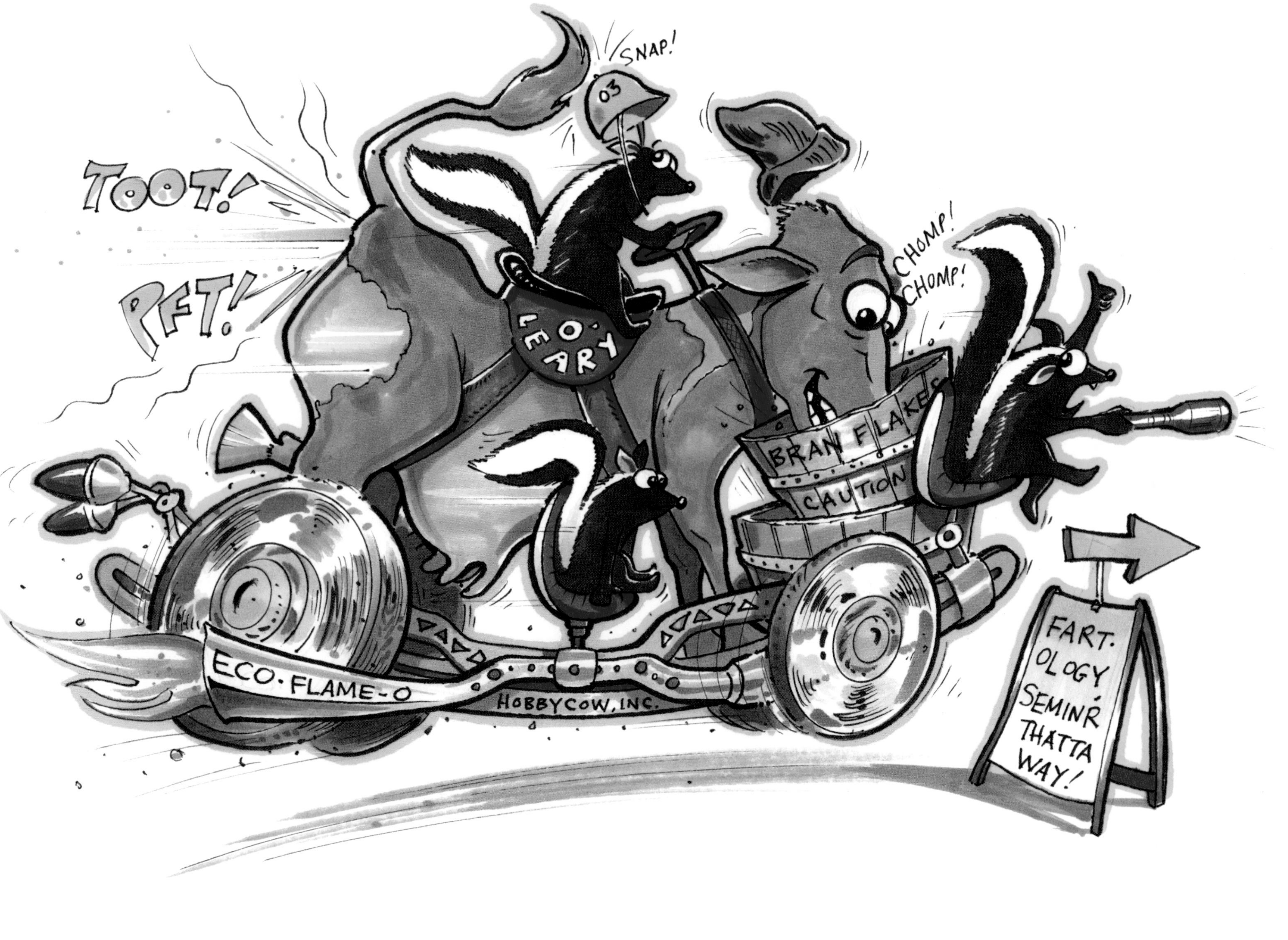
SNAP!
03
TOOT!
PFT!
O'LEARY
CHOMP! CHOMP!
BRAN FLAKES
CAUTION
ECO-FLAME-O
HOBBYCOW, INC.
FART-OLOGY SEMINR THATTA WAY!

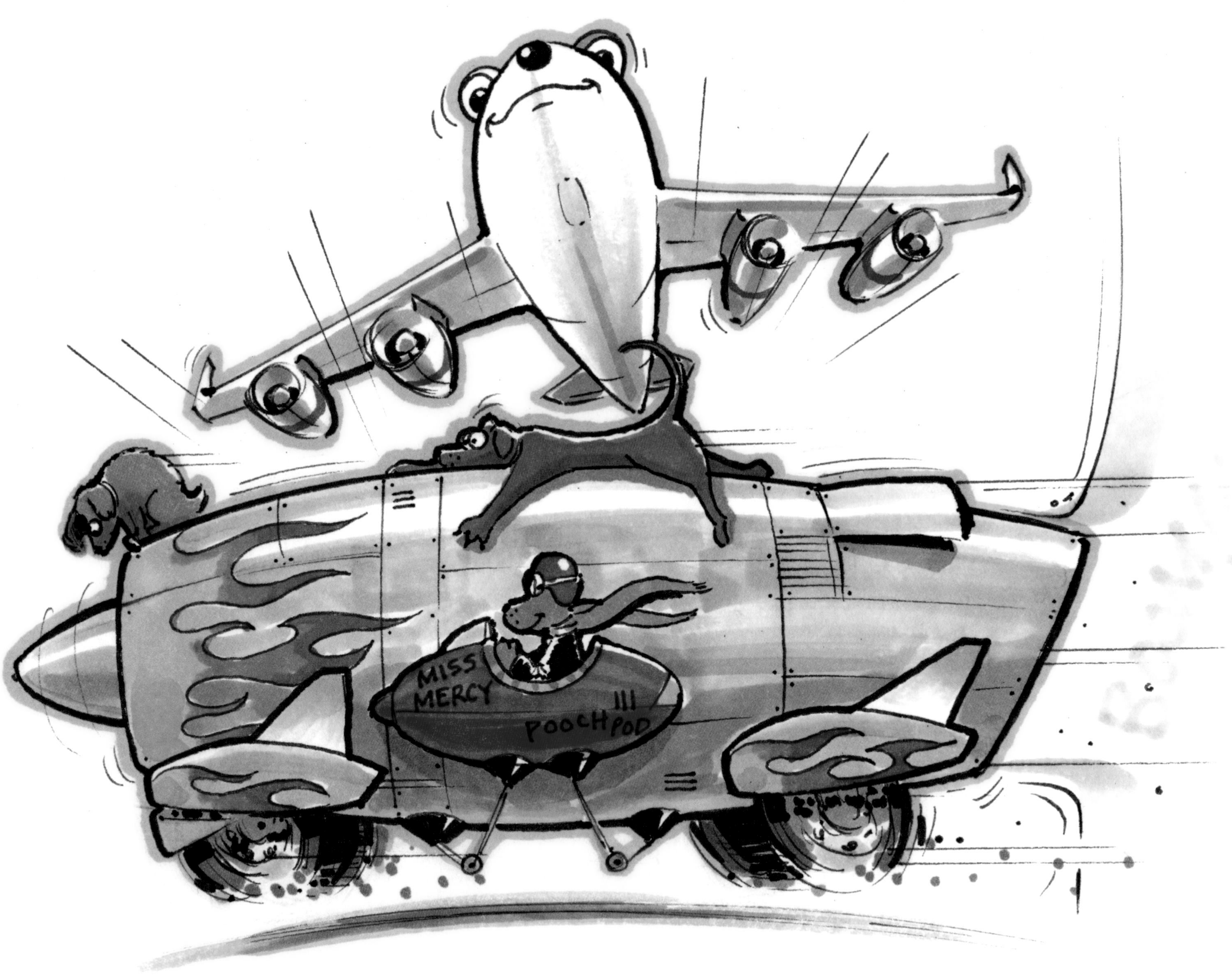
MISS MERCY
POOCH POD

FIREBALL TIM'S

"Hello."

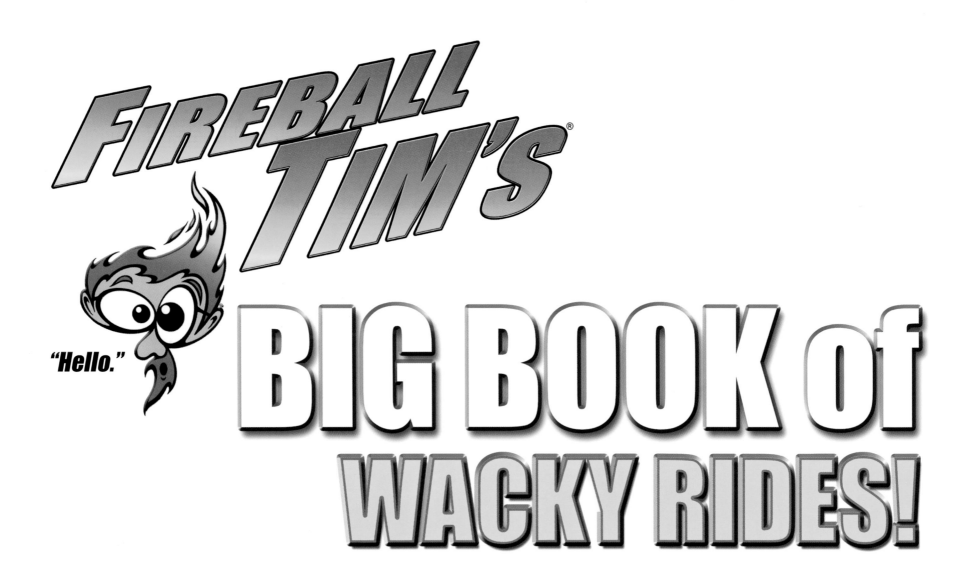

BIG BOOK of
WACKY RIDES!

designstudio|PRESS

BigB

"THE 4 ALARMSTER!"

In an emergency, these bugs know how to get things done quick! Not all Lady Bugs are ladies!

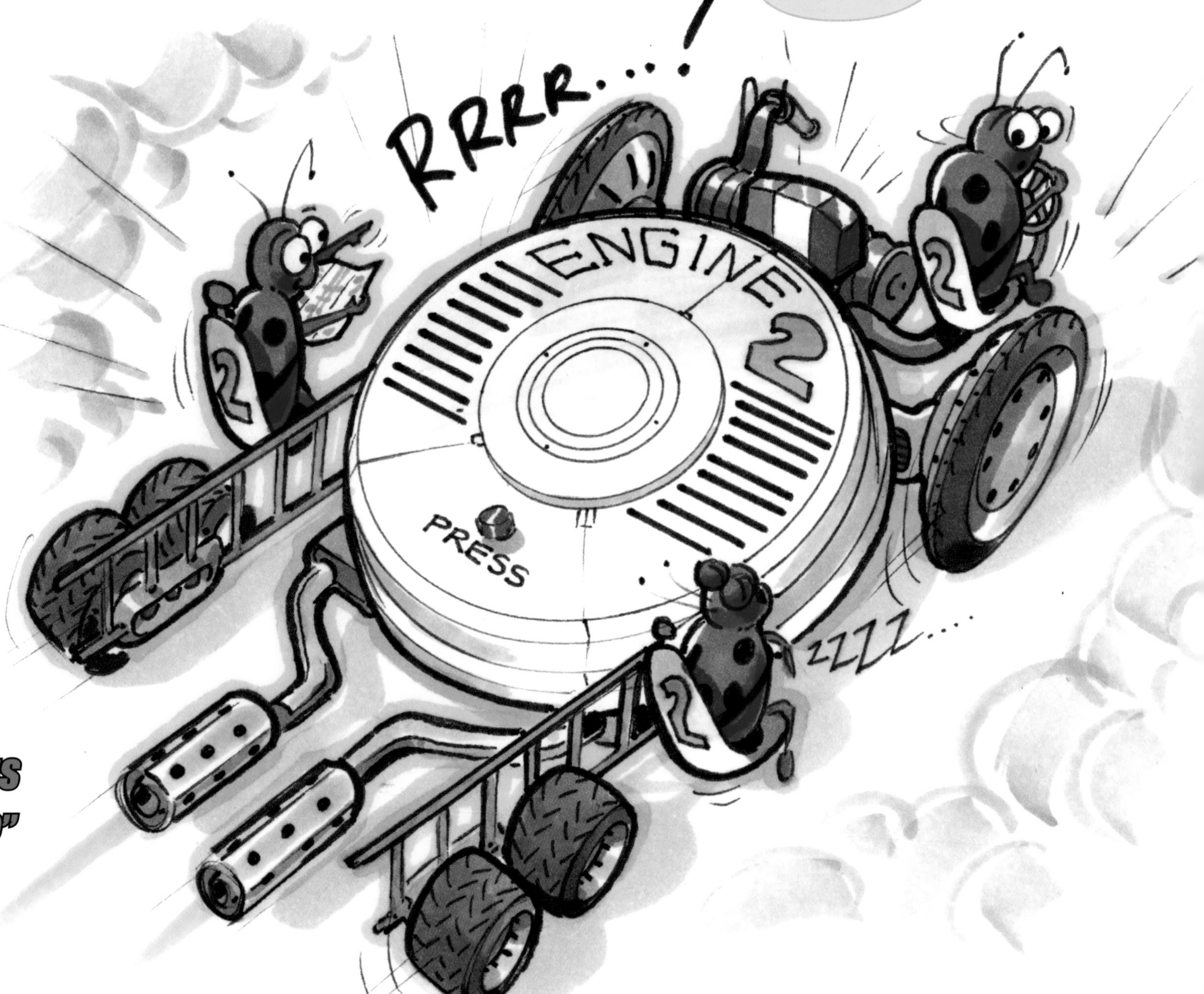
RRRR...!
ENGINE
2
PRESS
ZZZZ....

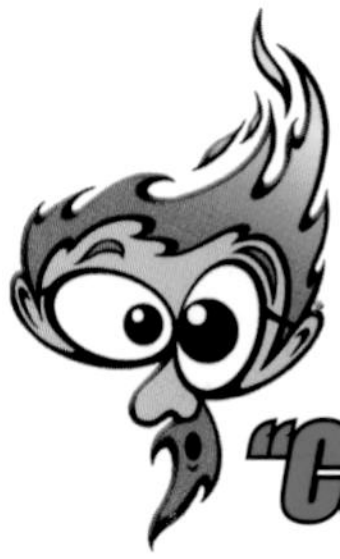

"Can you get things done quickly, too?"

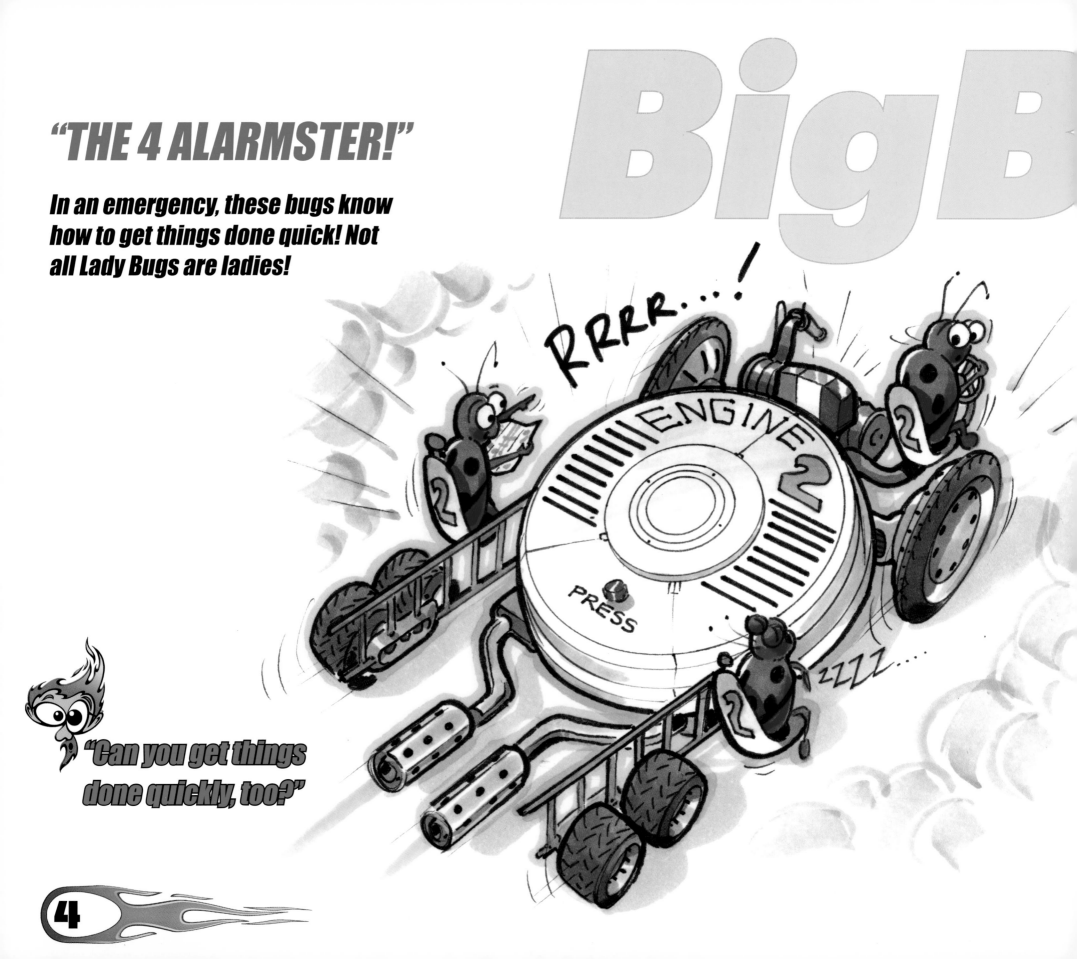

OOMERS

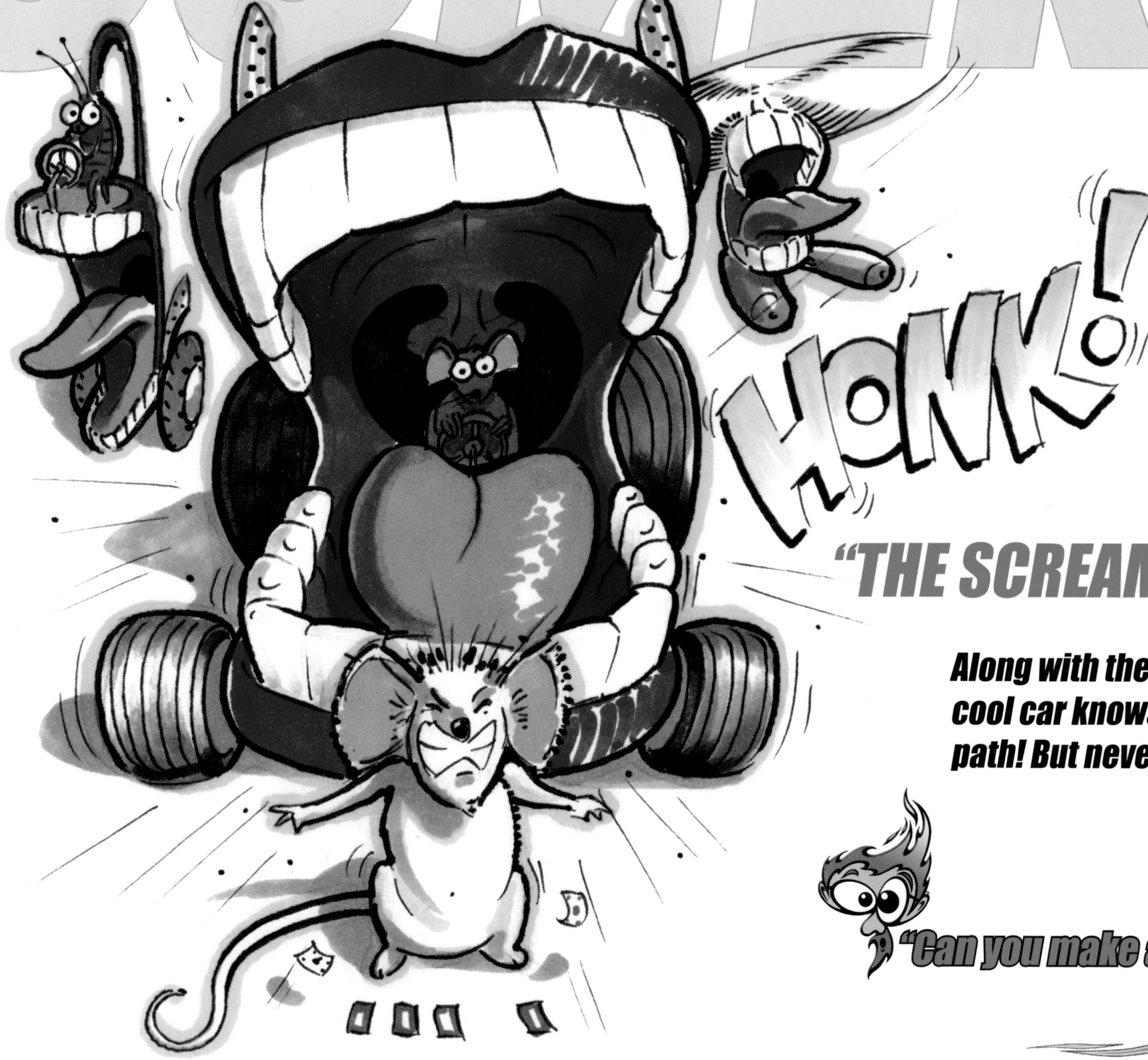

HONK!

"THE SCREAMINATOR!"

Along with the YELLICOPTER. This cool car knows how to clear a path! But never indoors!

"Can you make a honk sound?"

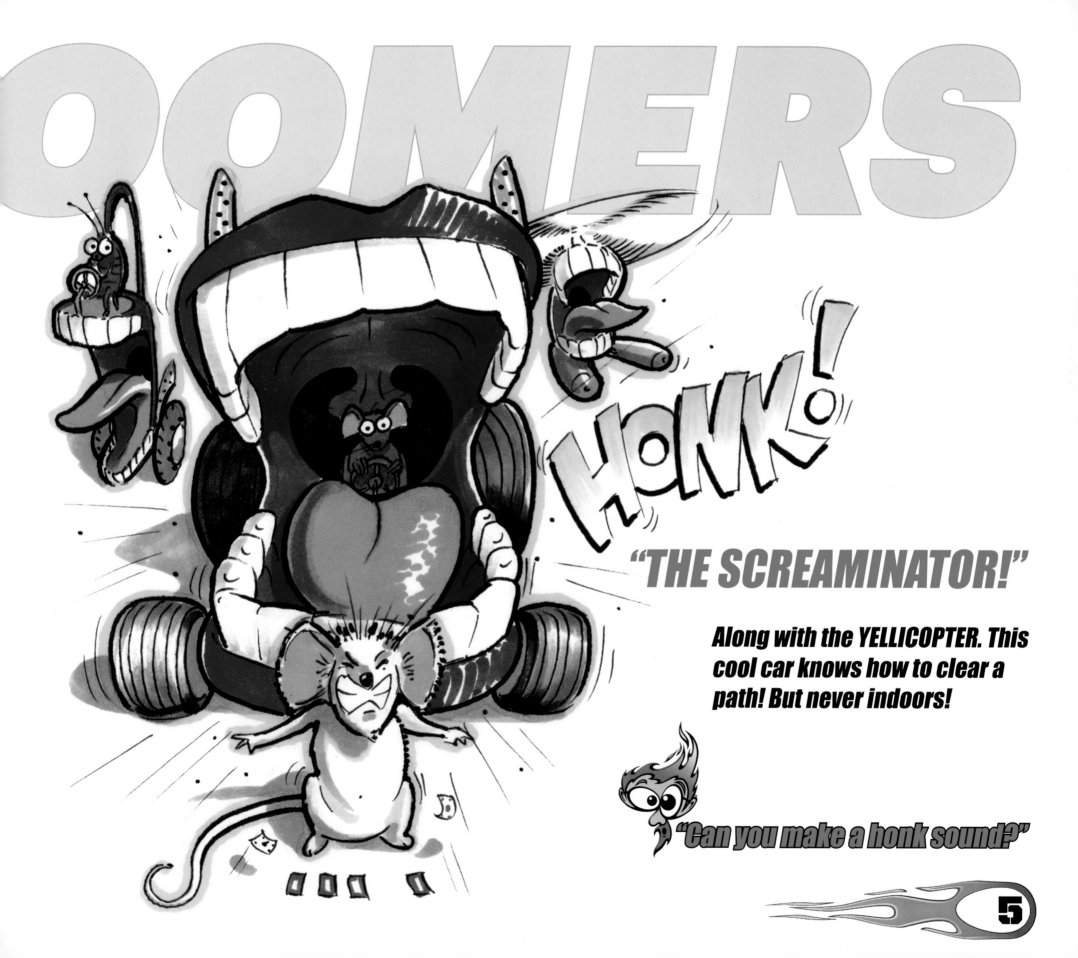

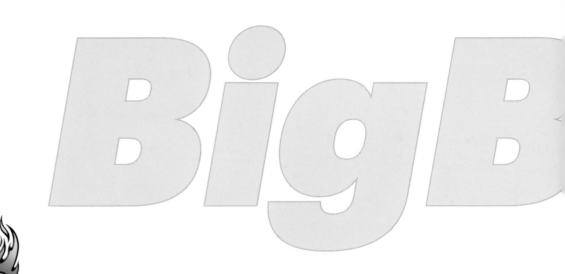

"THE SNOT ROCKET!"

Everyone has to blow their nose. But stand clear, or you're sure to get wet!

Big B

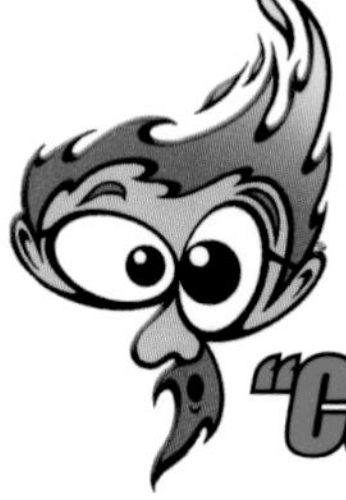
"Can you whistle through your nose?"

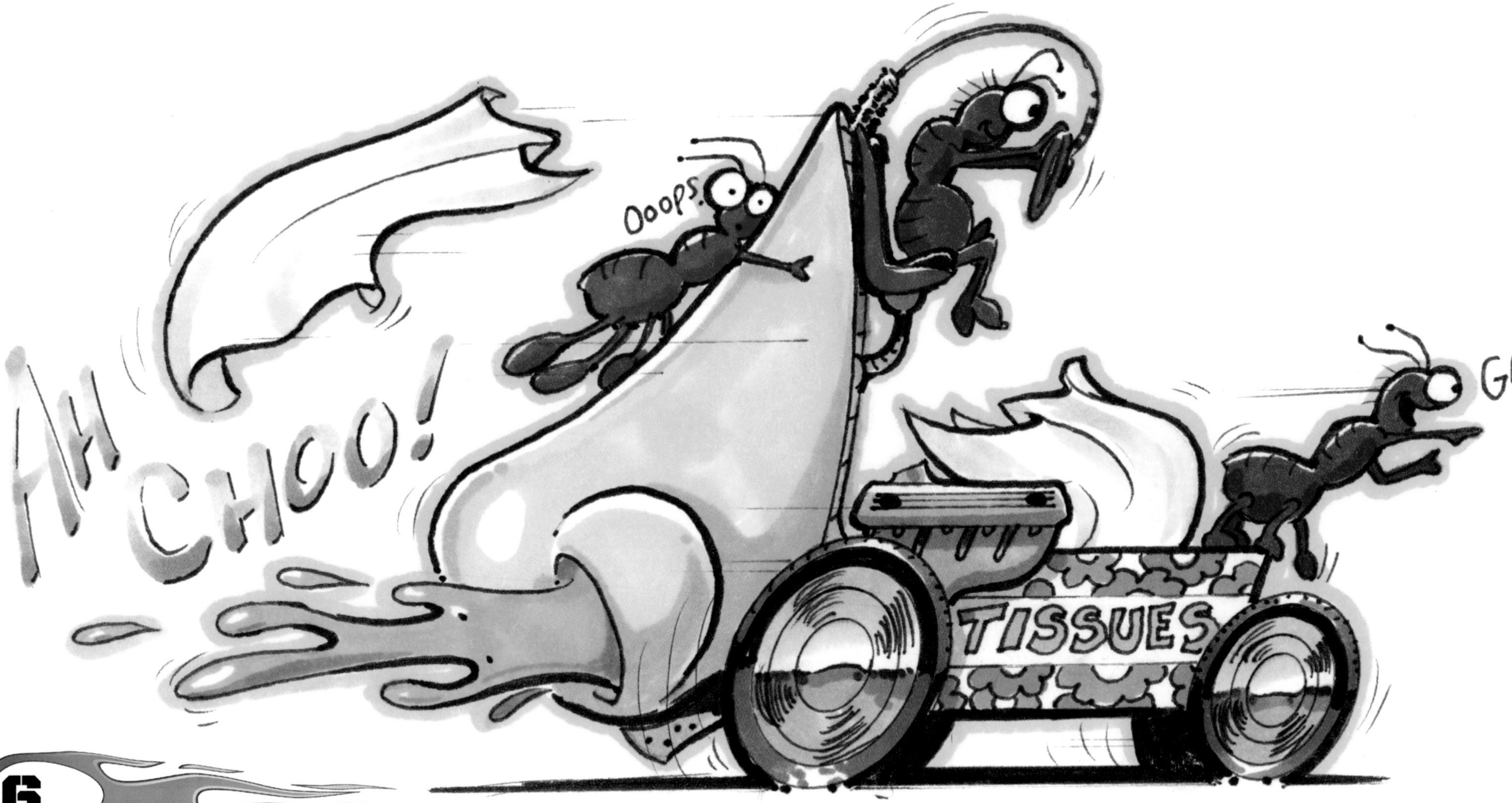
Ooops.
GO!
AH CHOO!
TISSUES

OOMERS

"FLYIN' FREDDY'S TIME JUMPER!"

Freddy's jumps are always on time! And that's important when you're a frog.

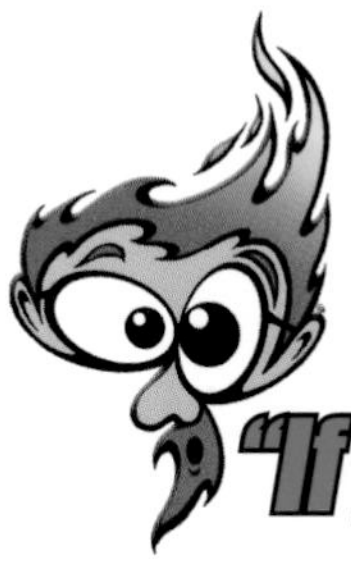

"If you had a frog, what would you call it?"

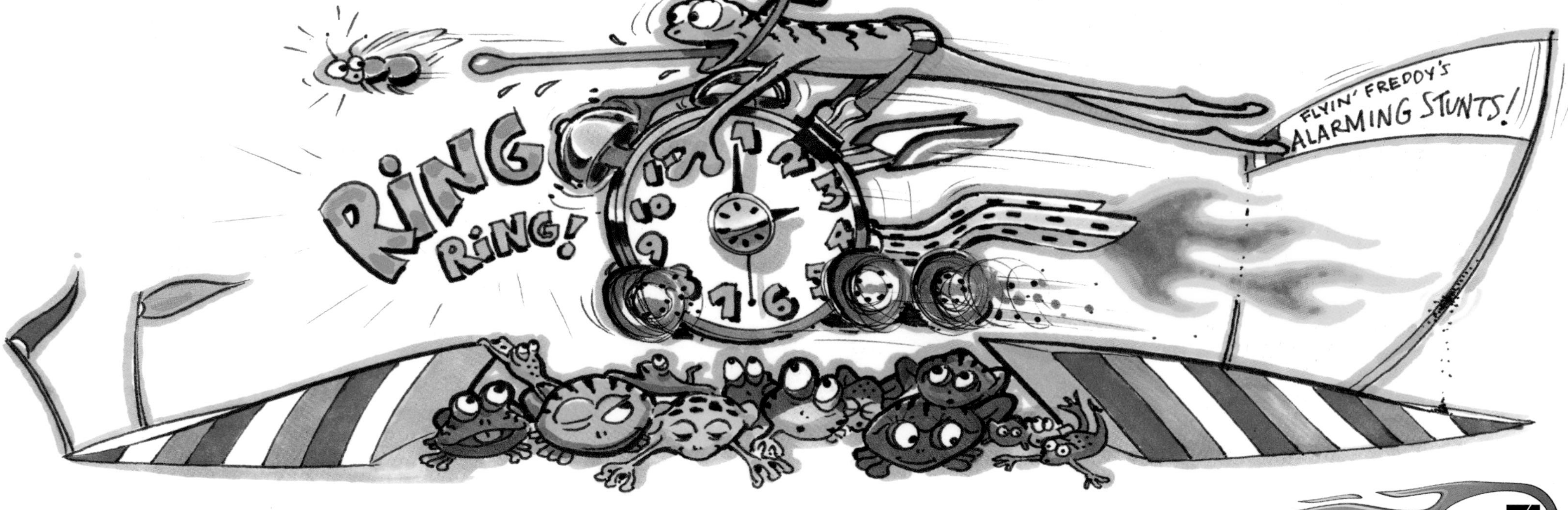
RING
RING!
FLYIN' FREDDY'S
ALARMING STUNTS!

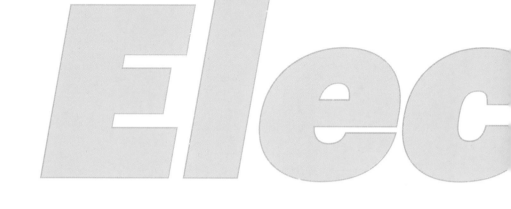

"BUG AND SAMMY'S CARPET LAYING MACHINE!"

Bug and Sammy love carpets to play on, so they invented their own machine.

"What kind of machine can you invent?"

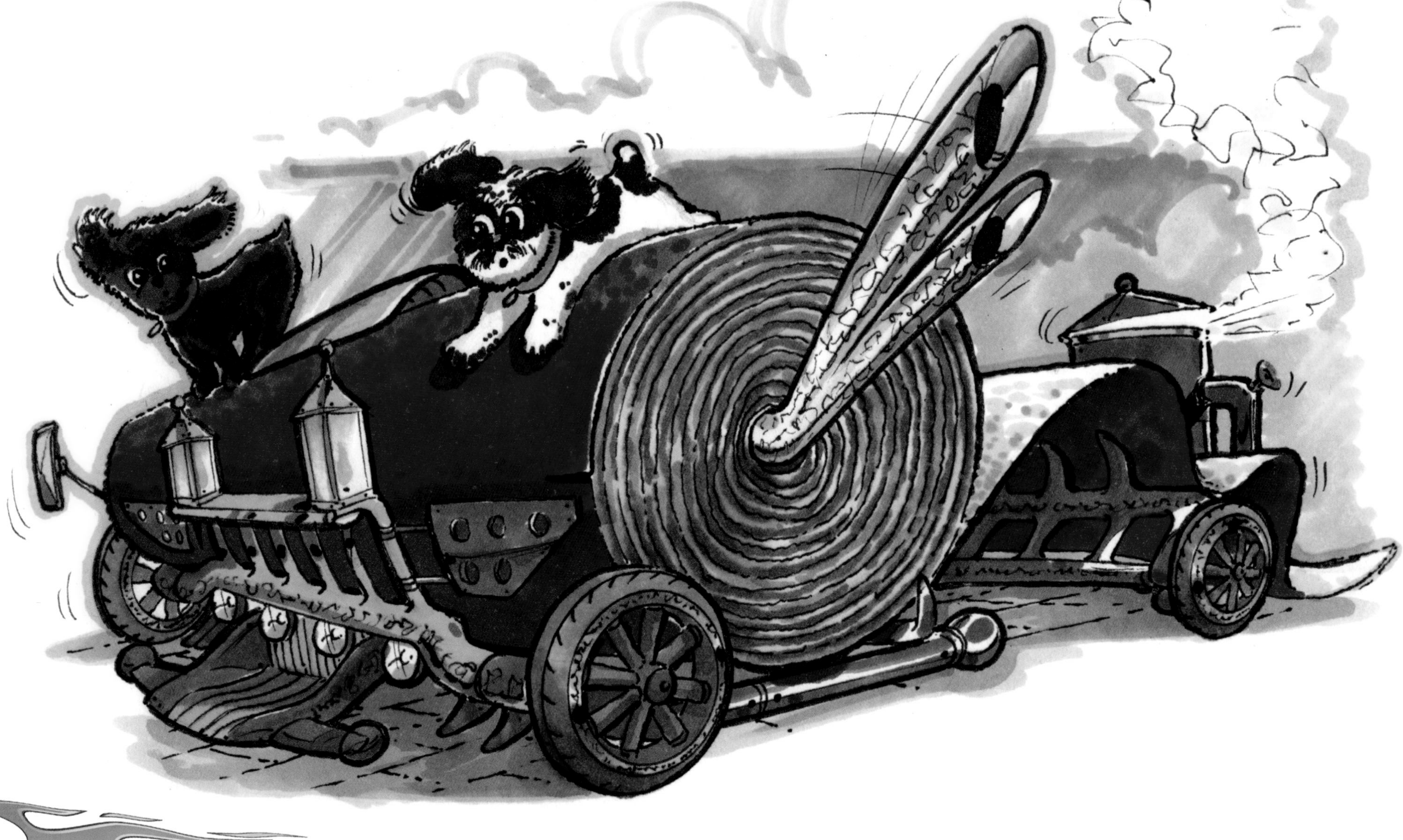

Elec

TRICKS

"WILLY THE WEASEL'S POWER PACK!"

Willy always knows where to go to get fully charged. Because batteries never work unless they are!

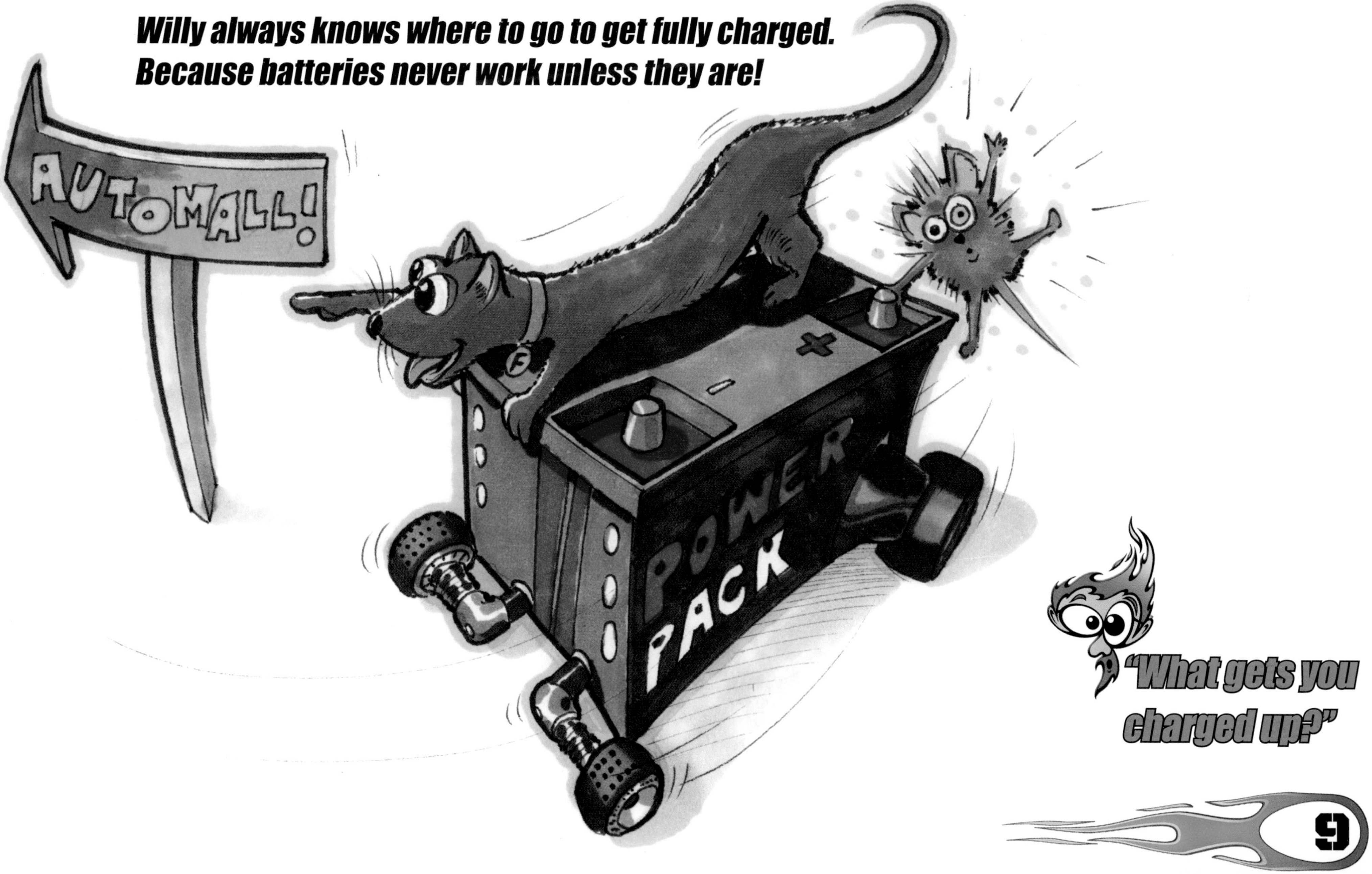

AUTOMALL!
+
-
F
POWER
PACK
"What gets you charged up?"

Elec

"THE TELEPHONE POLLSTER!"

Phone polls may not last much longer, but they make cool cars thanks to this family of pigeons.

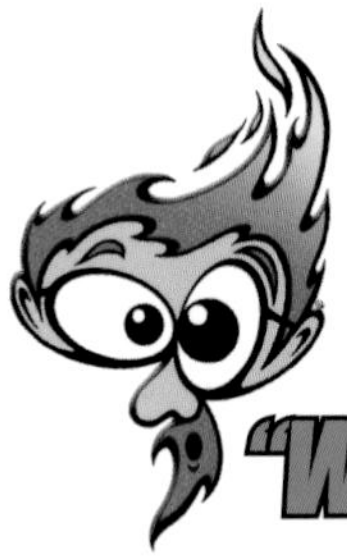

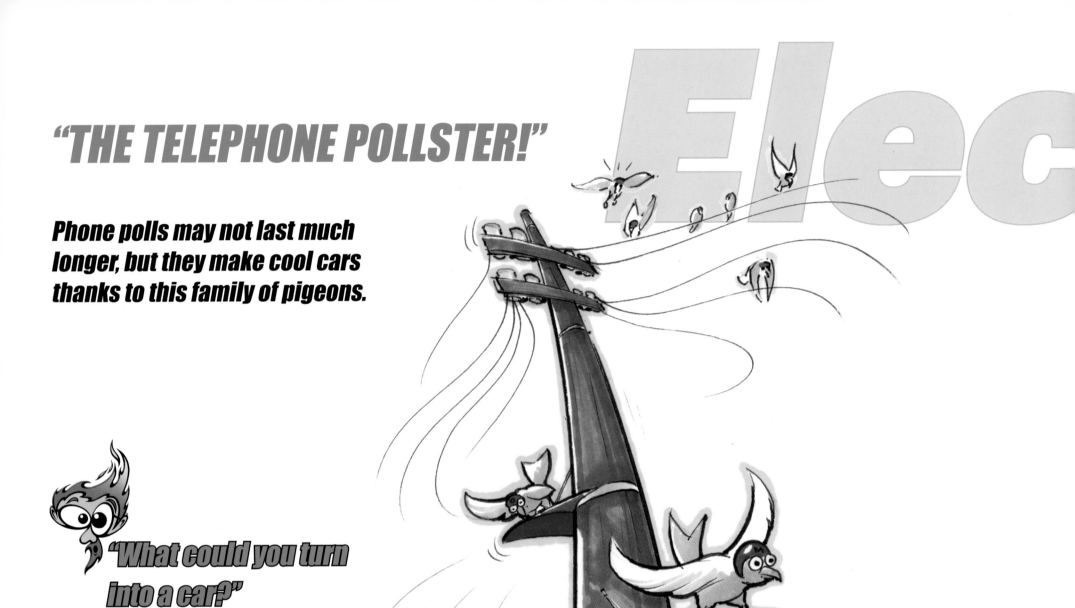

"What could you turn into a car?"

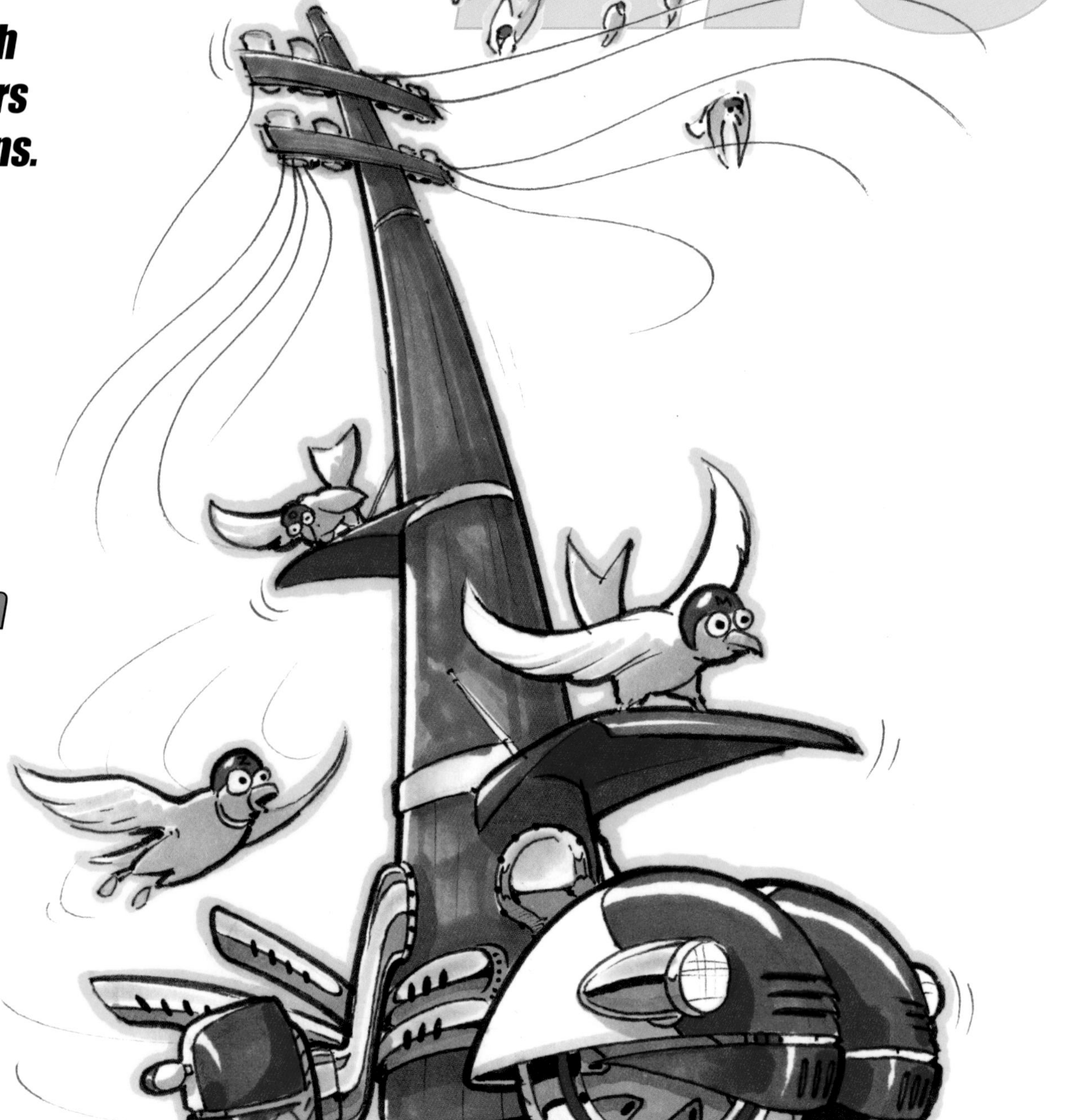

TRICKS

"SNAKESTRIP!"

These lil' snakes bring electricity wherever they go. But you have to be careful not to get shocked! Ouch!

Electricity lights up THE WHOLE WORLD.

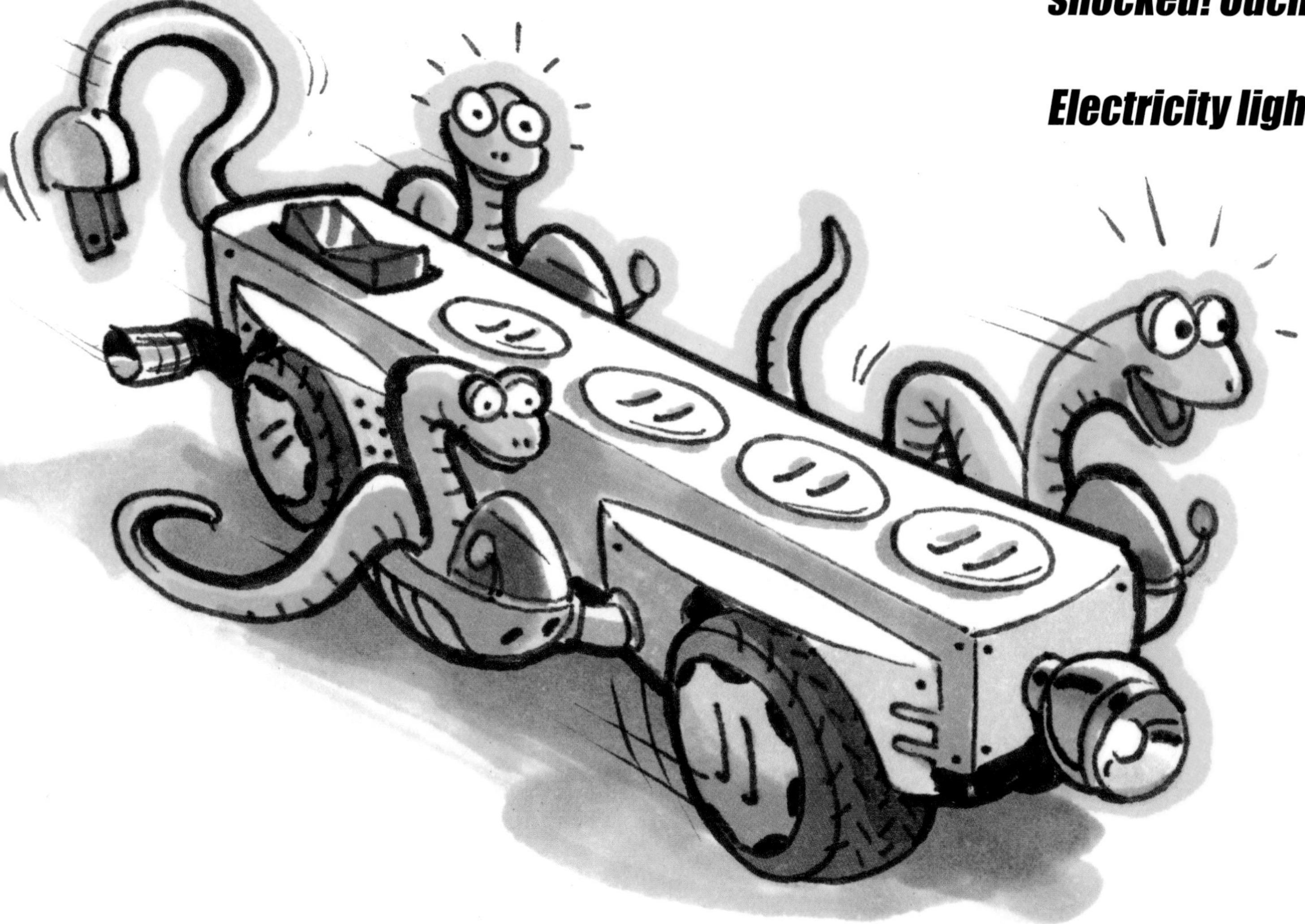

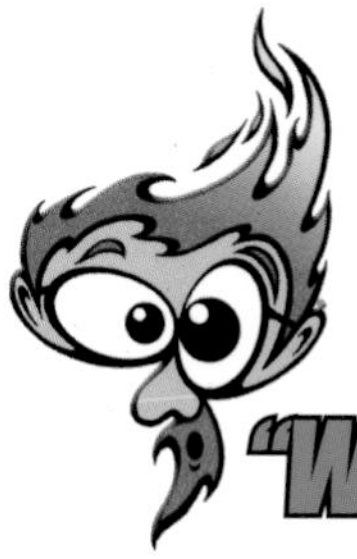

"What does it light up in YOUR house?"

Elec

"SOLAR SAM!"

Sam loves the sun. And being a Hedge Hog, he gets plenty of time to travel.

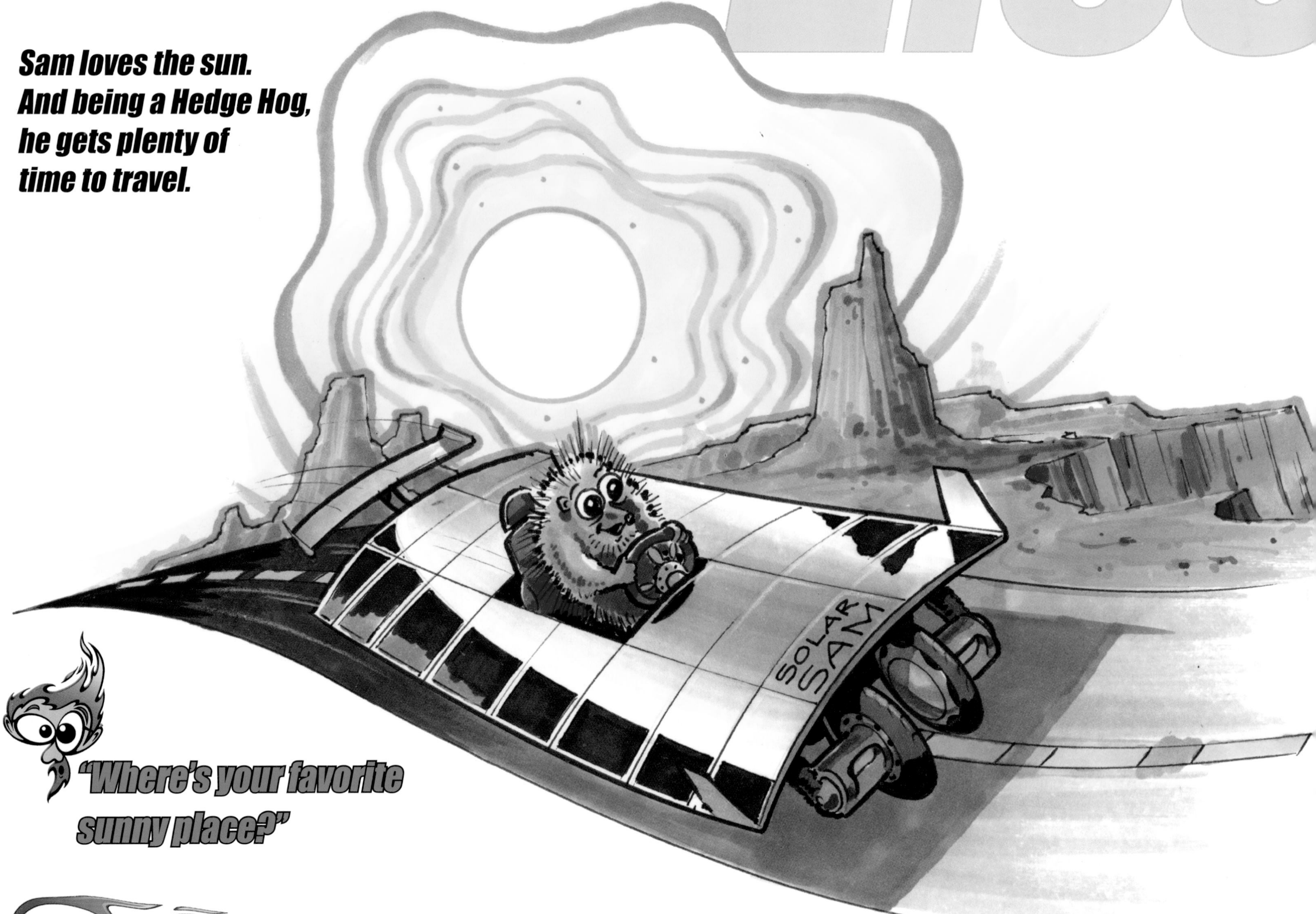
SOLAR SAM

"Where's your favorite sunny place?"

TRICKS

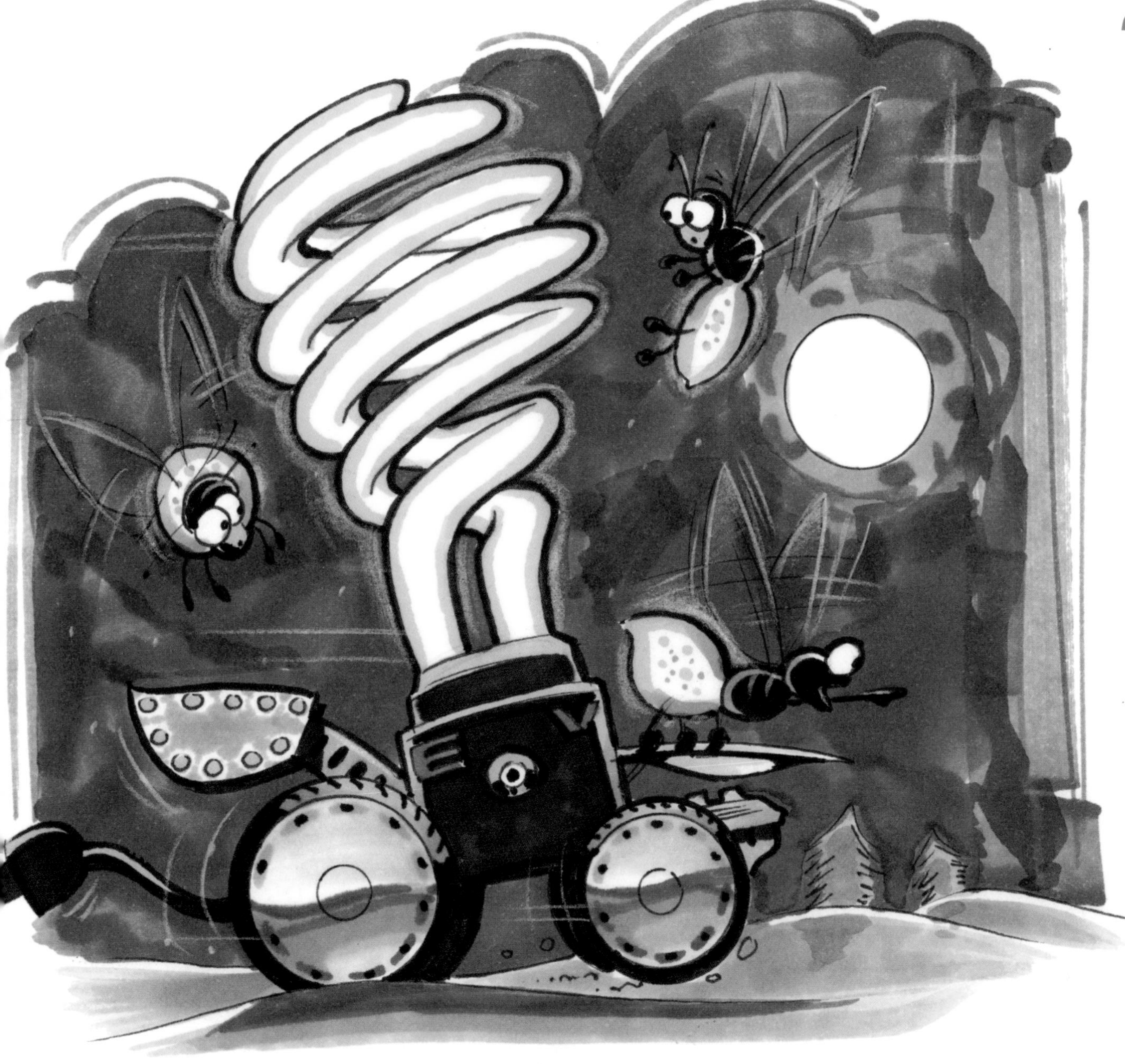

"THE BULBINATOR!"

Even Lightning Bugs can use a little help. And with this cool Lightbulb Hot Rod, they can rest and save their energy.

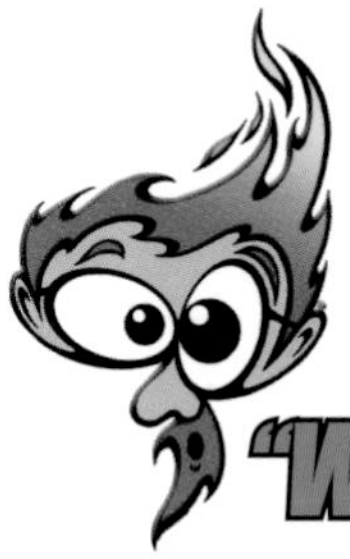

"What are some ways that you can save energy?"

Huge

"ZERMATTSTER!"

It's the biggest and the baddest! A mountain of a car, this goliath makes his own roads.

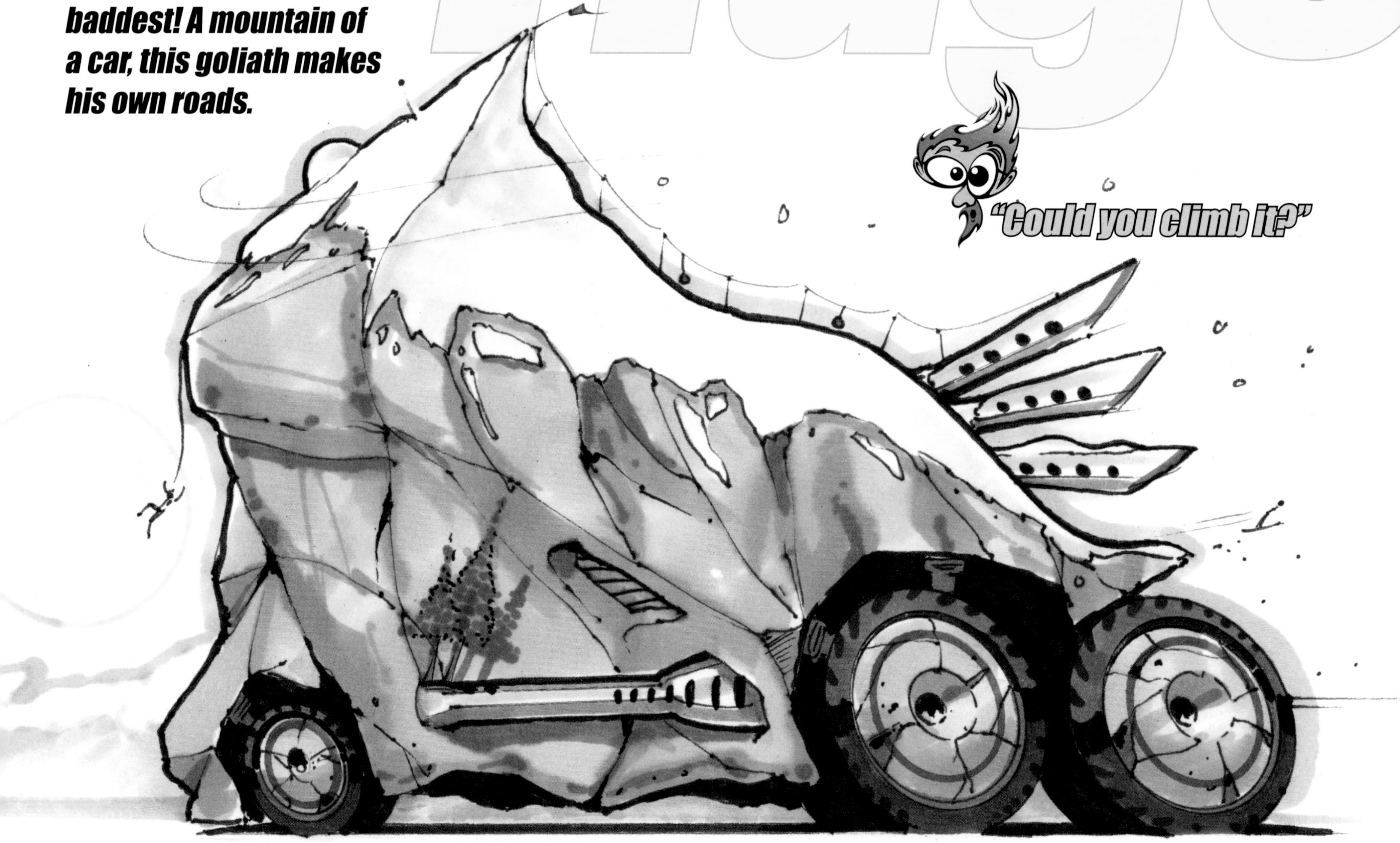
"Could you climb it?"

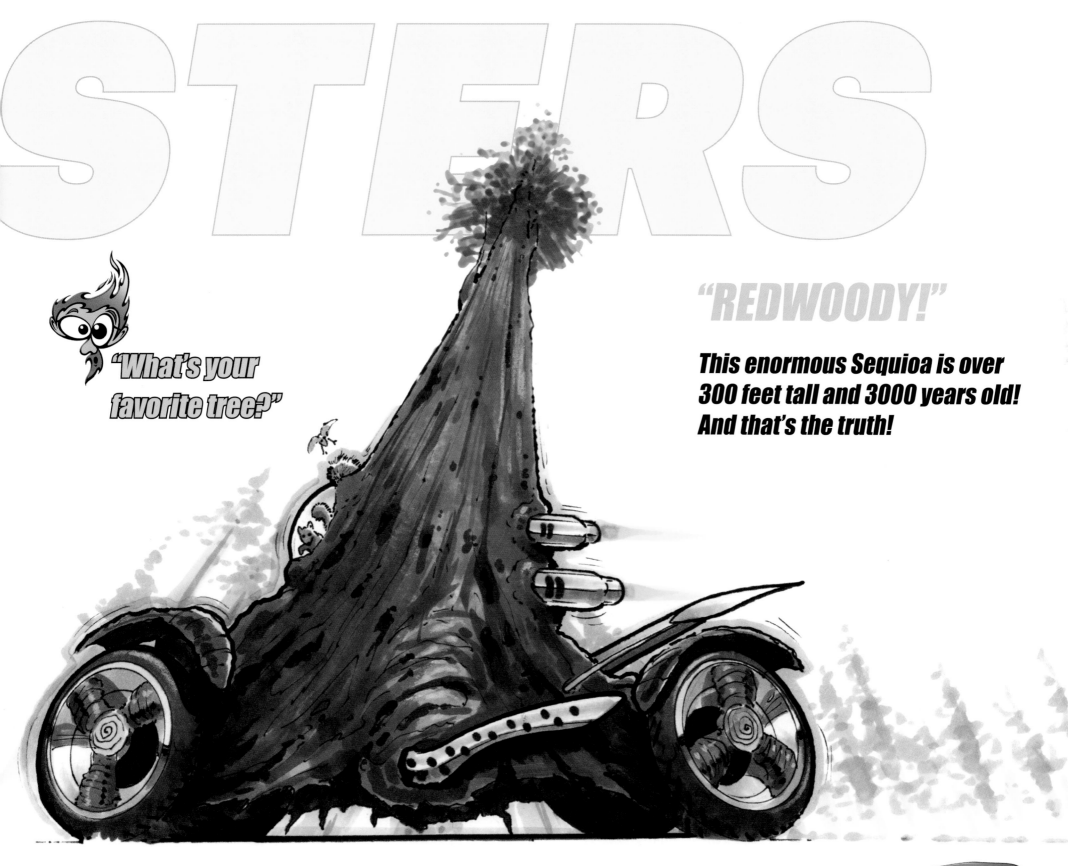

STERS

"What's your favorite tree?"

"REDWOODY!"

This enormous Sequioa is over 300 feet tall and 3000 years old! And that's the truth!

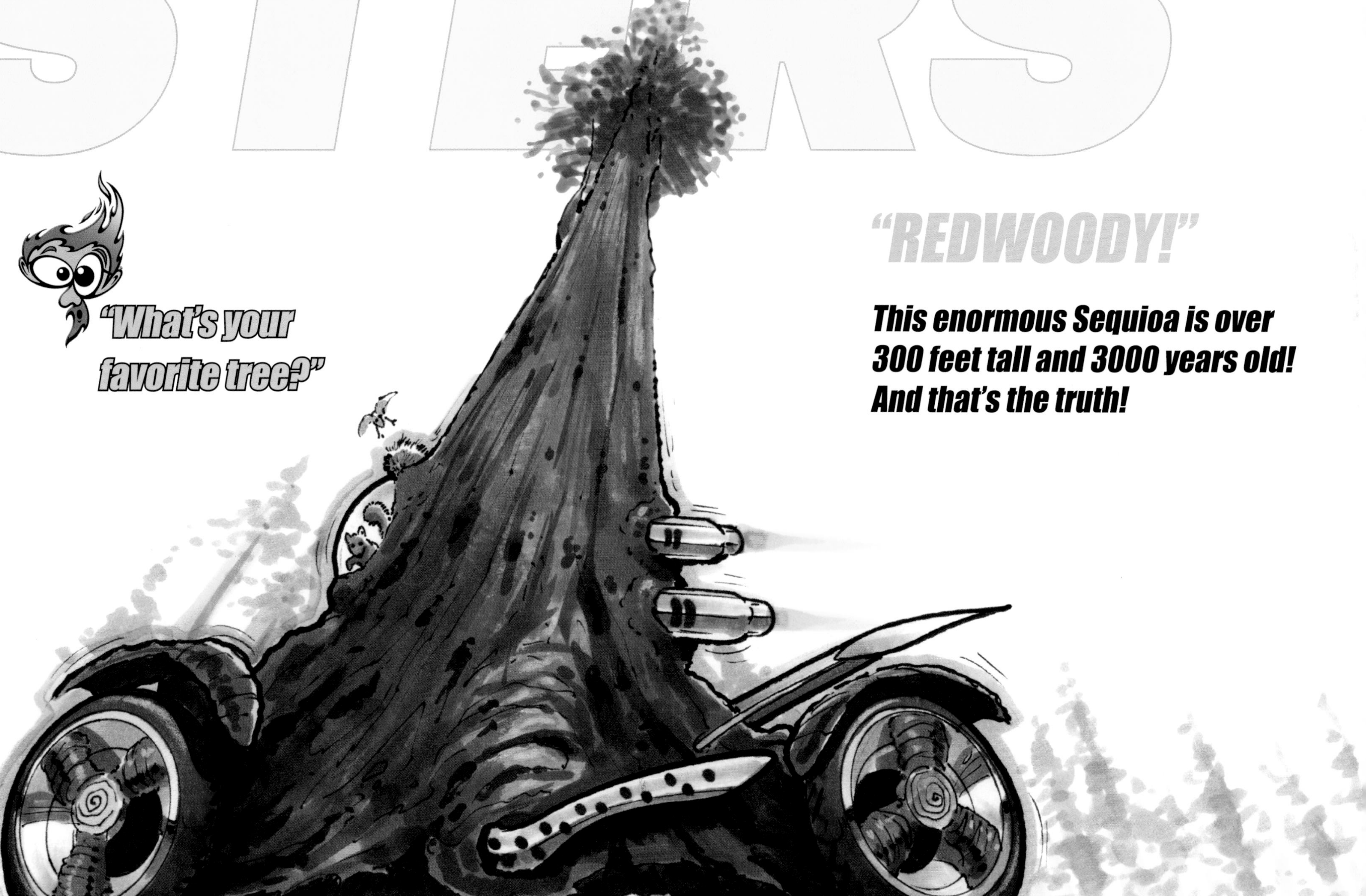

"COOL CORP!"

One of the biggest Hot Rods on the planet, Cool Corp stands for all things cool. And it's a 100% green vehicle!

Huge

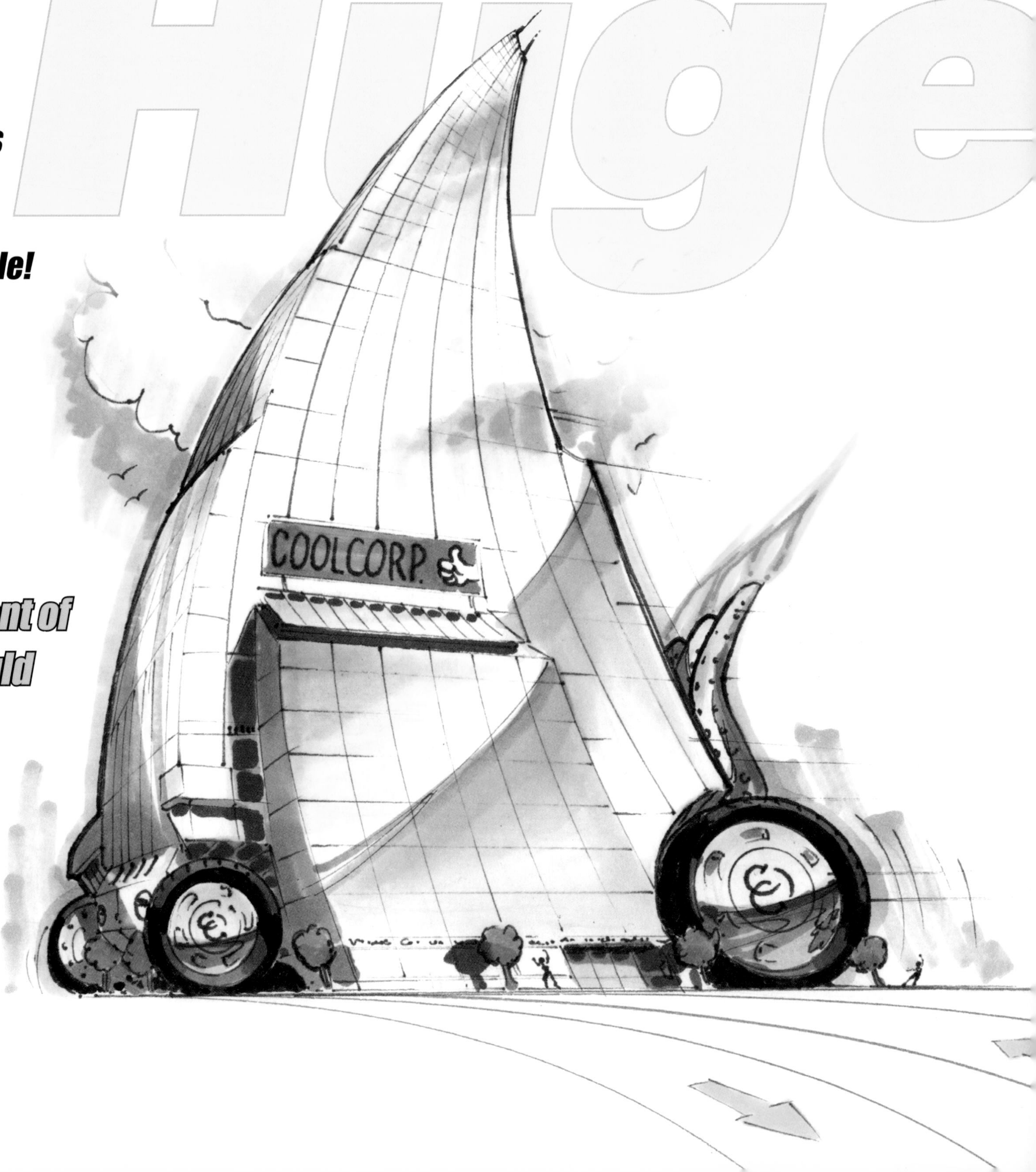
COOLCORP.

"If you were President of Cool Corp, what would you do?"

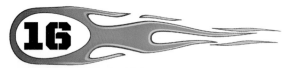

STERS

"KING CRUISER!"

Not only huge, but this rocket can go just as fast in the water!

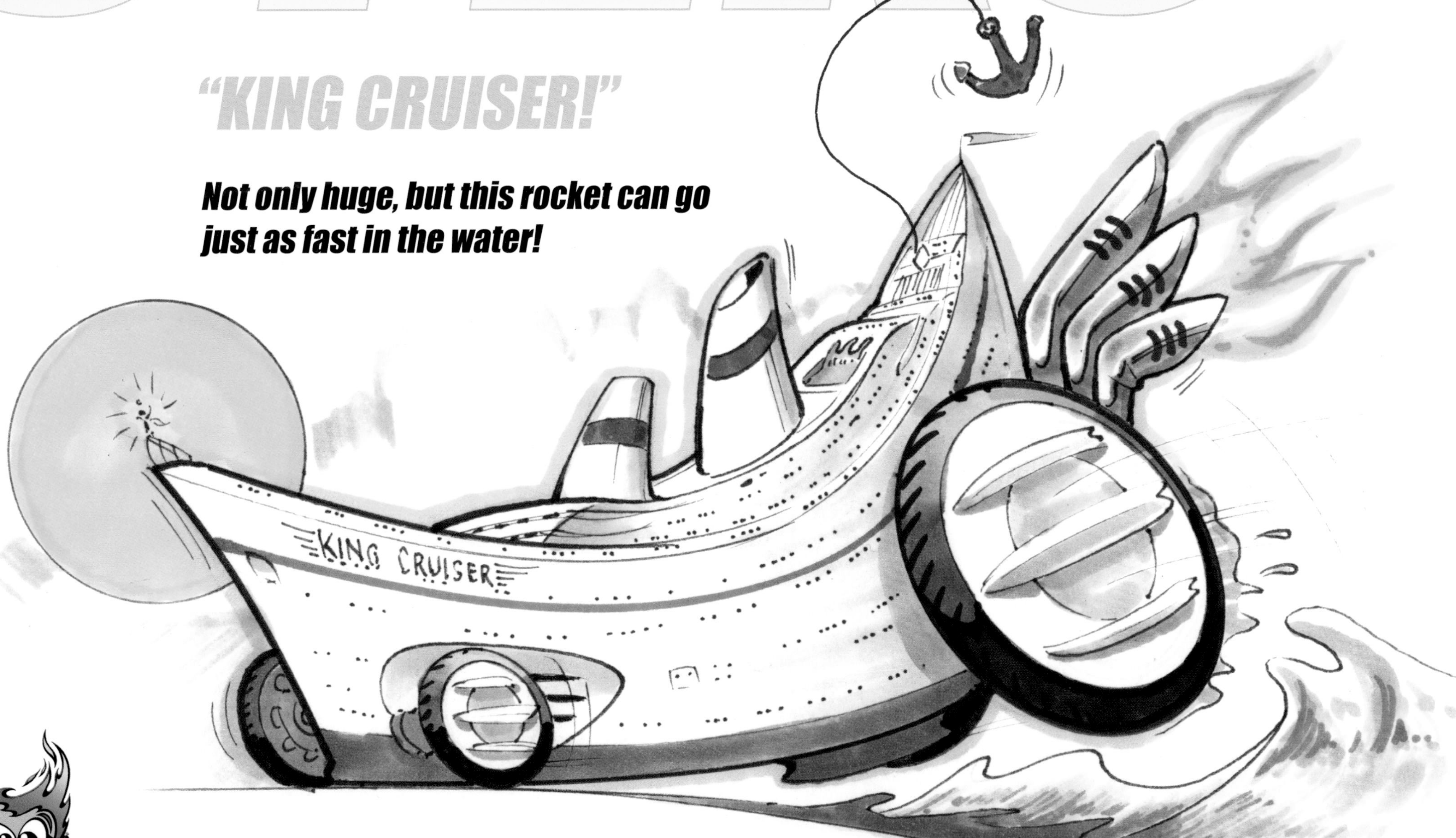
KING CRUISER

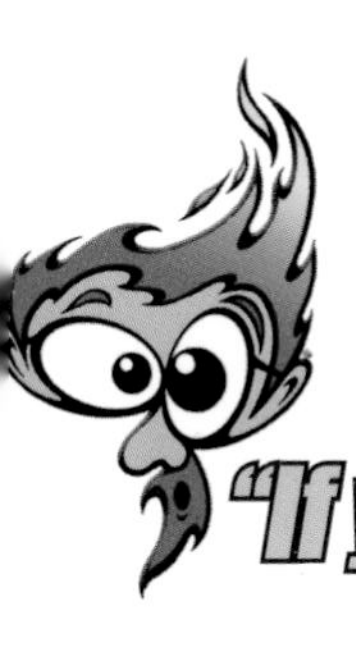

"If you were captain of King Cruiser, where would you go?"

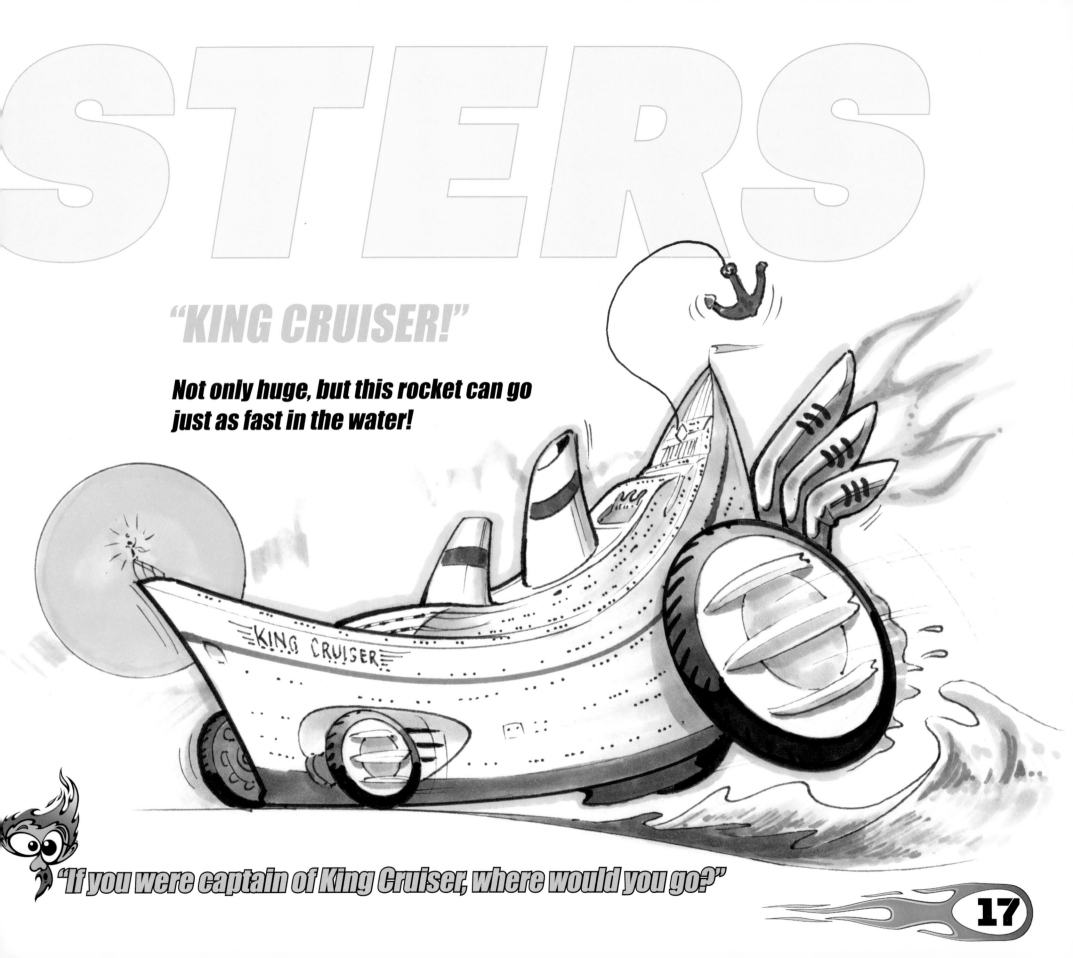

"THE SHELLINATOR!"

Carl the Crab loves to race, and his Shellinator is one of the fastest.

"What's your favorite kind of race car?"

FREE TEST DRIVE! TODAY ONLY

4 SALE 1 OWNER

RACERS

"MAC'S CHEESEY DRAGSTER!"

Careful to keep your eye on your Mac n' Cheese, or it might take off!

"What do you like to have for dinner?"

Tiny

"THE SPOONSTER!"

Leroy the Lizard loves the Olympics. And with his Spoonster, he wins just about every event.

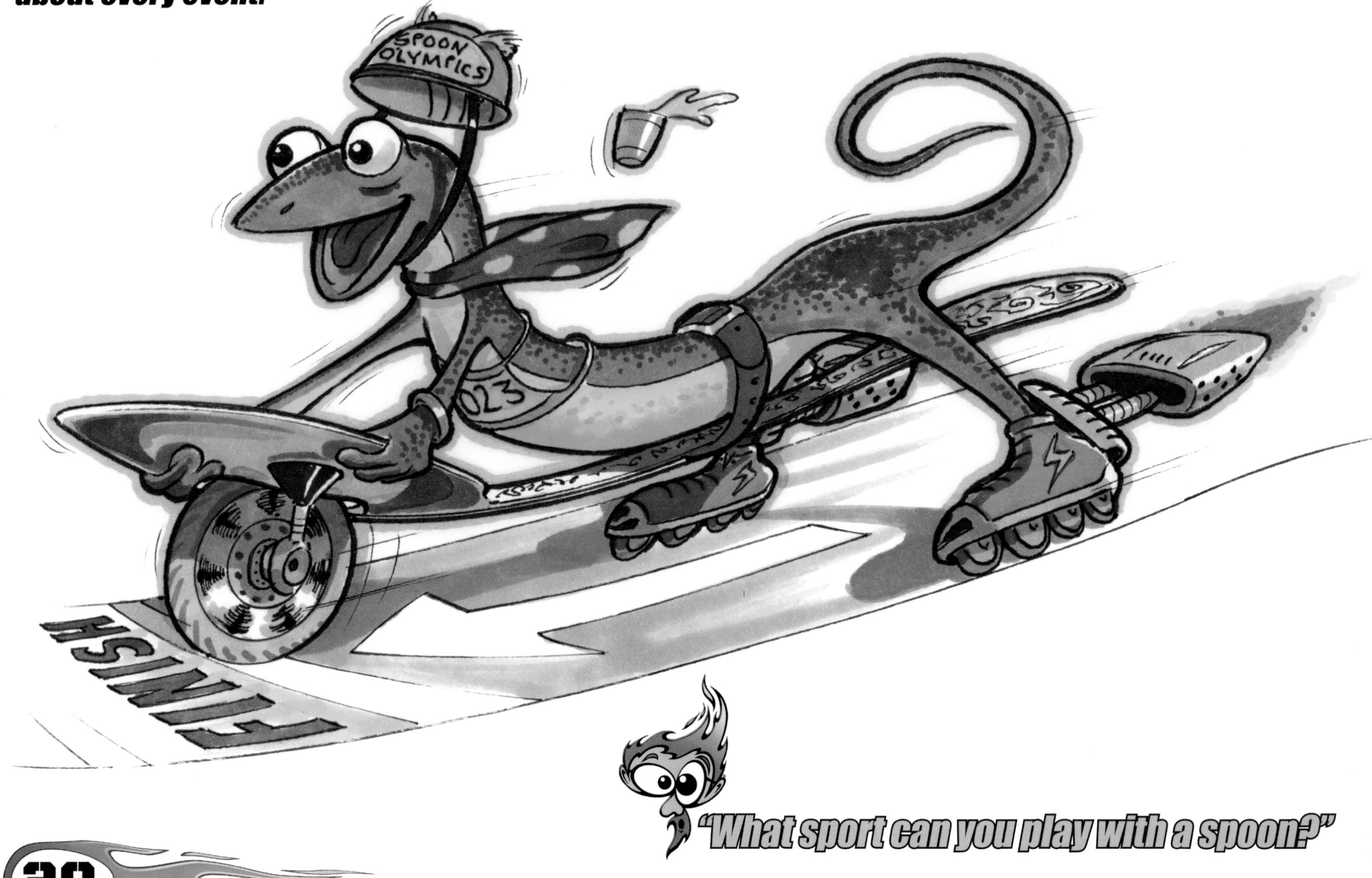
SPOON OLYMPICS
023
FINISH

"What sport can you play with a spoon?"

RACERS

"THE GALOW ROCKET!"

The Pepperoni Brothers love to go fast. So, they head to Bonnyville where they can test their cool rocket car safely. And, make some pizza.

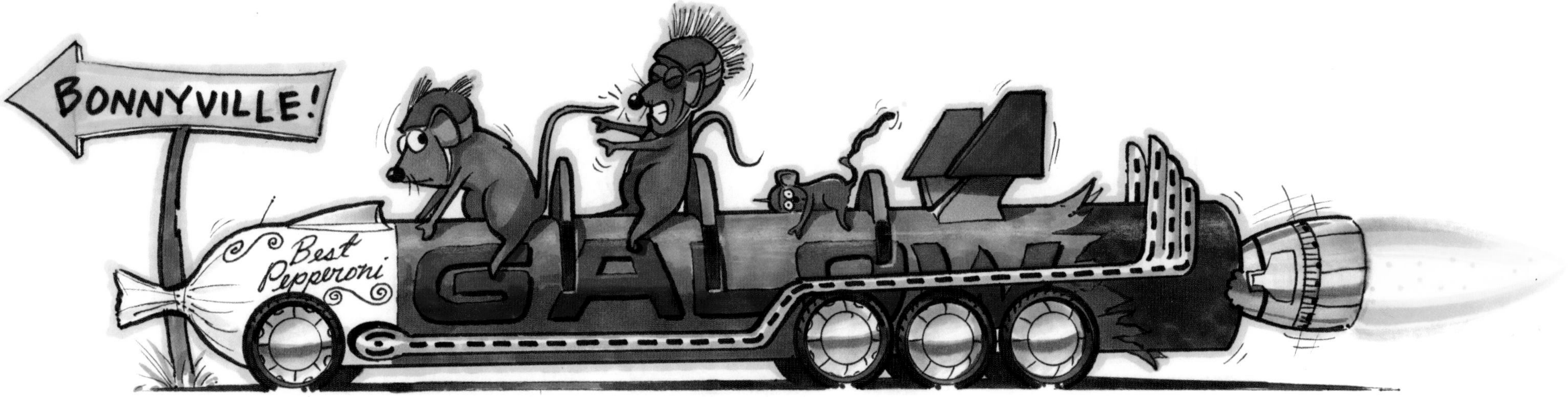

BONNYVILLE!
Best Pepperoni
GAL

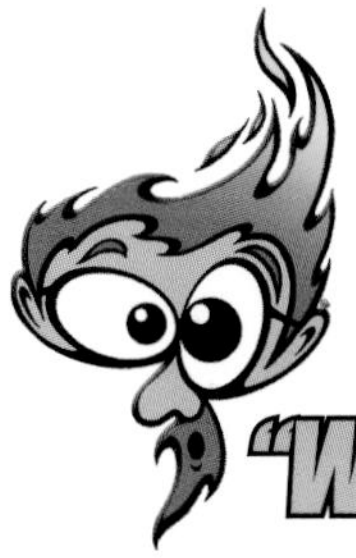

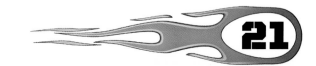

"What's your favorite pizza topping?"

Teeny

"RINGTONER!"

This is Caspar the Kangaroo Mouse who loves to talk. So he turned his old cell phone into a car! What a way to recycle!

TALK
DRIVE
RING!

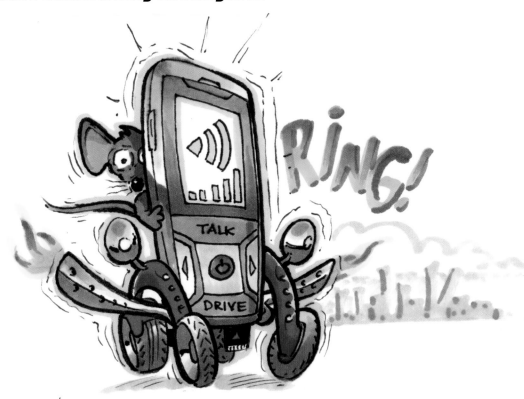

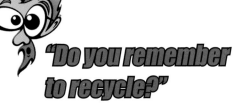

"Do you remember to recycle?"

PUT! PUT!
BOO BOOS
REPAIR BOOK

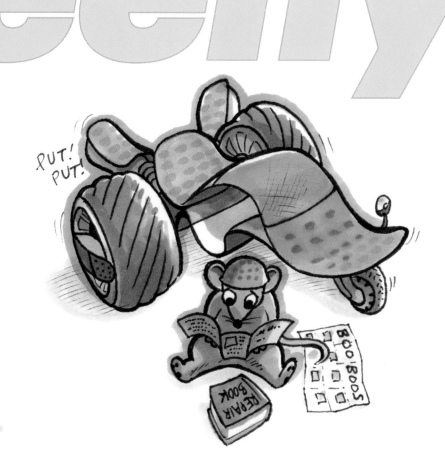

"BOO BOO MOBILE!"

When you have an ouchy, then this cool car will come to the rescue. As long as its driver can figure out how to make it go!

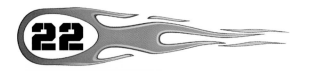

"Are you wearing a Boo Boo Mobile right now?"

ROCKETS

"THE CORKSTER!"

This is Pappy. And he loves to ride Corks when they pop! Although, the landing can be rough!

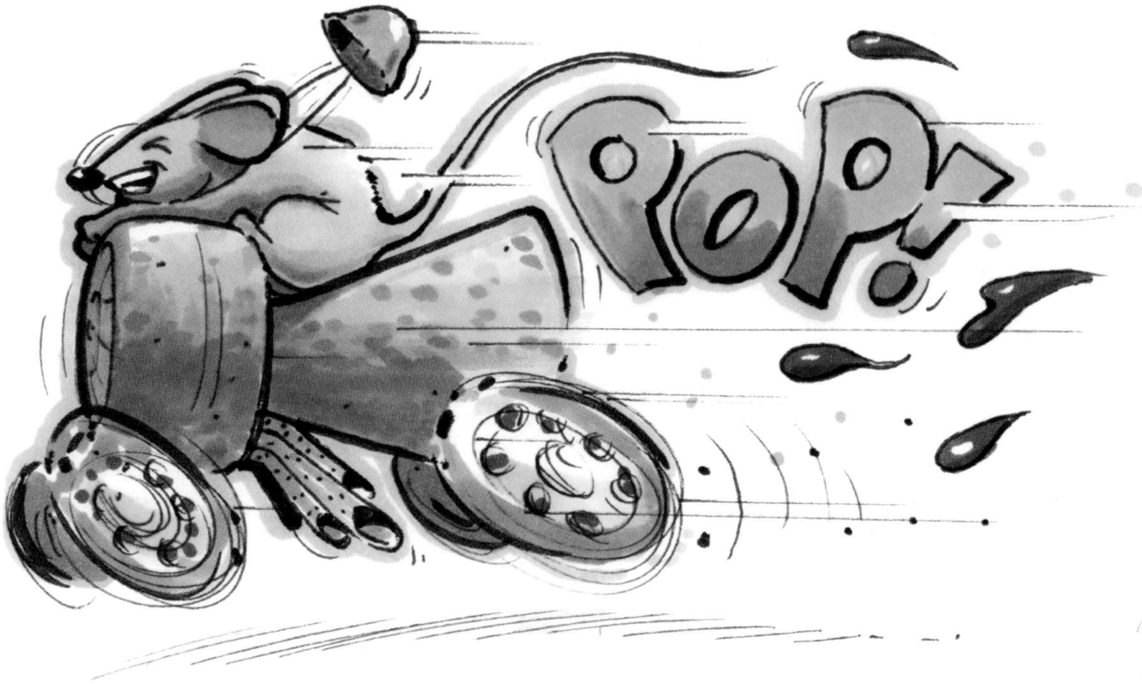
POP!

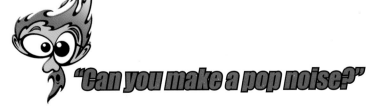

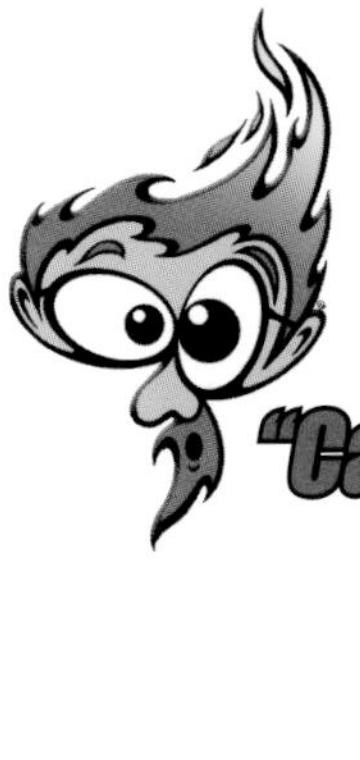
"Can you make a pop noise?"

"PENNYSIDE RACER!"

Give a penny for every penny you get, and watch them grow just like Mary the Mouse does! She's smart and loves to share.

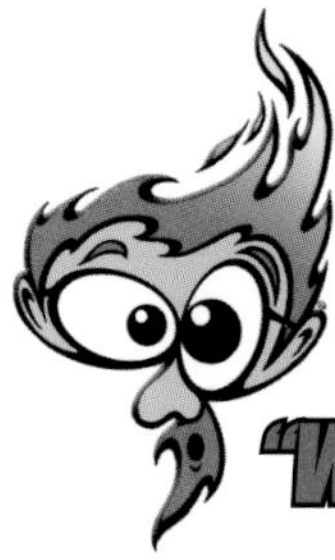
"Who can you give a penny to?"

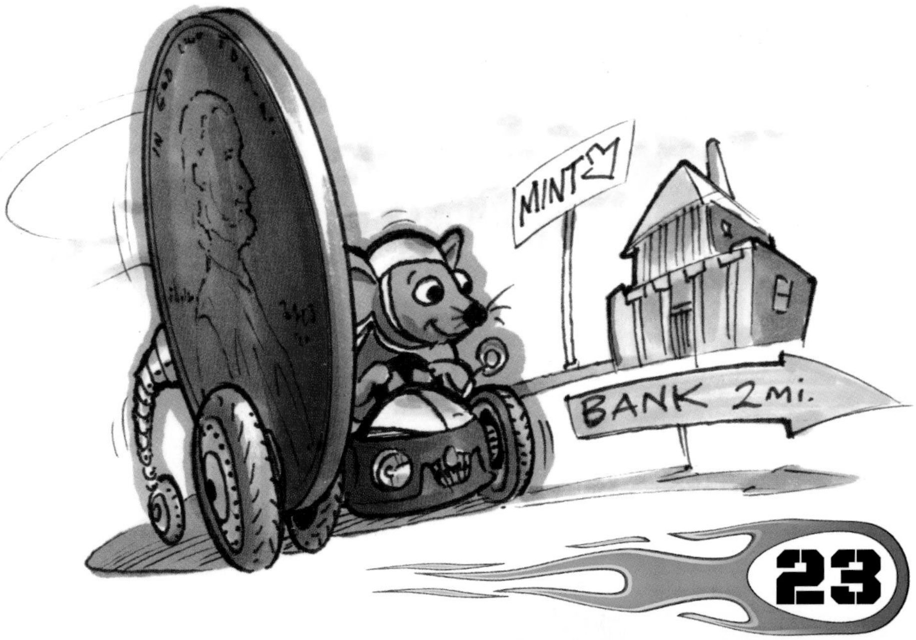
MINT
BANK 2mi.

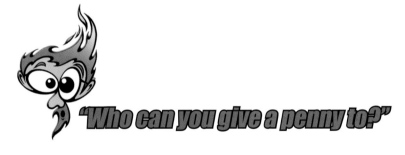

Teeny

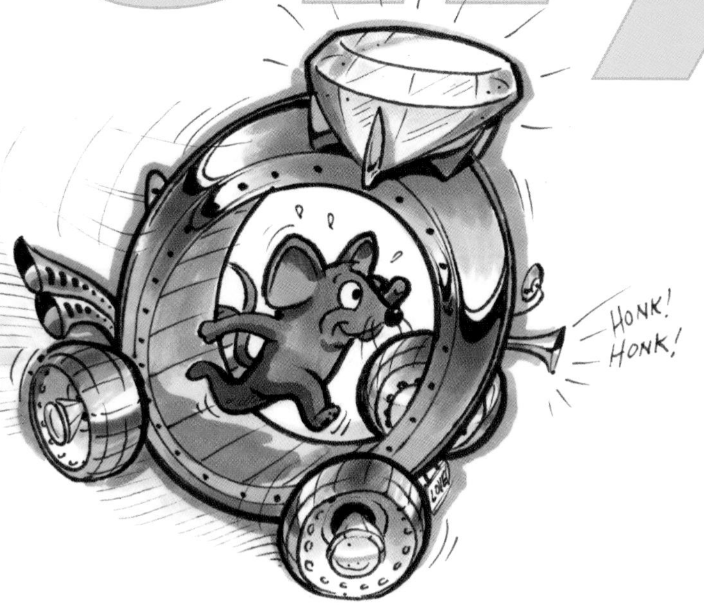
HONK! HONK!

"JAVA JAMMER!"

This coffee powered Hot Rod gets its power from the coffee maker!

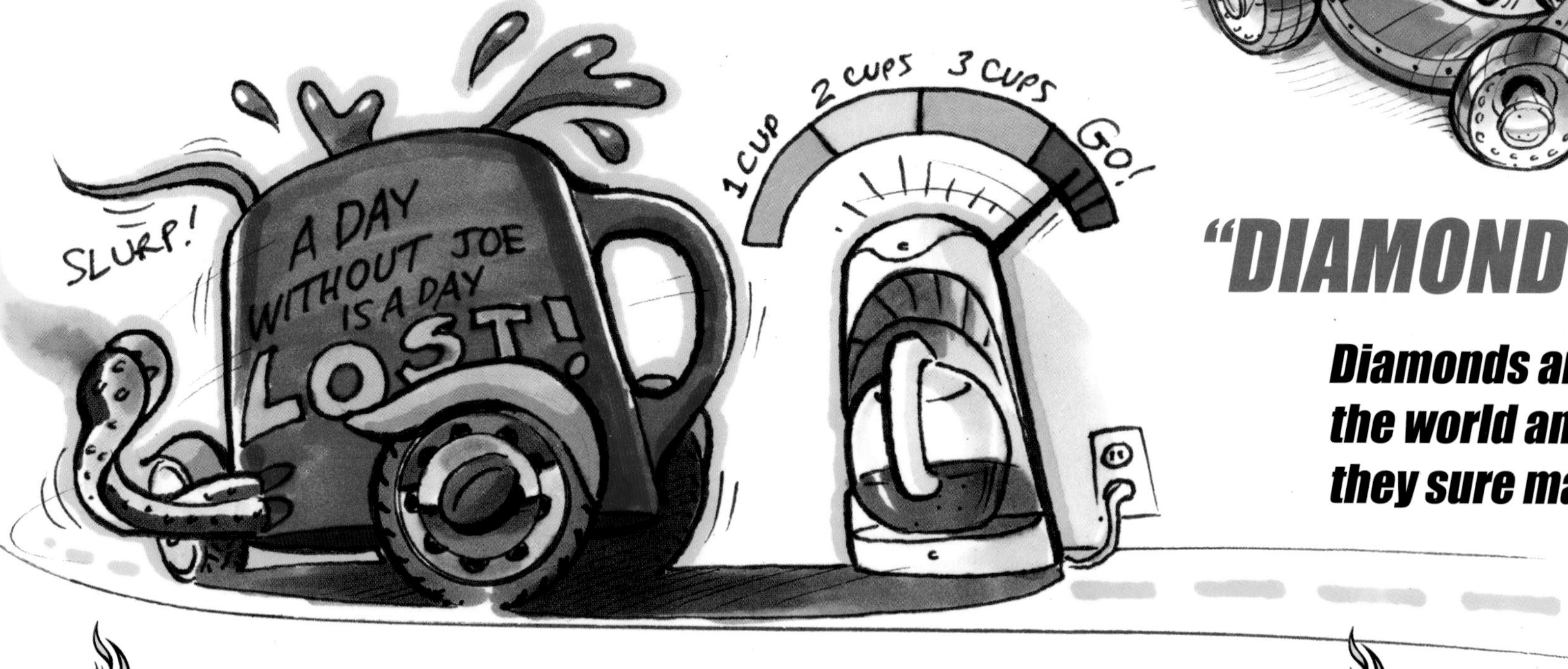
SLURP!
A DAY WITHOUT JOE IS A DAY LOST!
1 CUP
2 CUPS
3 CUPS
GO!

"DIAMOND RINGSTER!"

Diamonds are the hardest thing in the world and very beautiful, but they sure make cool cars, too!

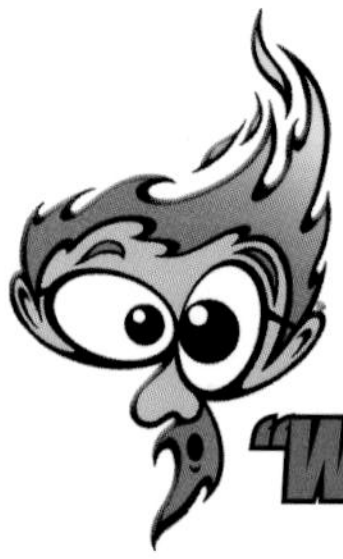

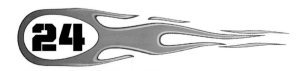

"Where do you get your power from?"

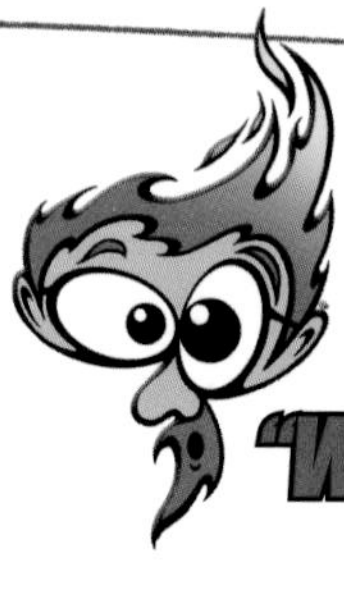

"What else is beautiful?"

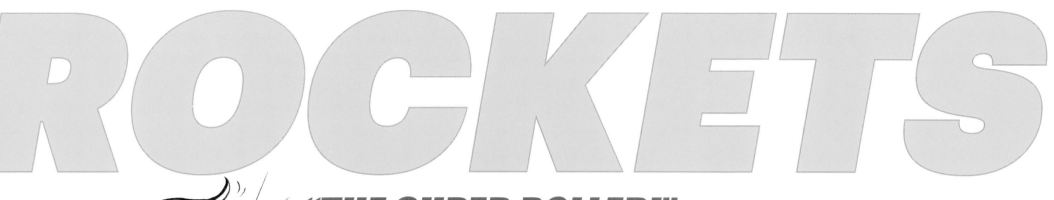

ROCKETS

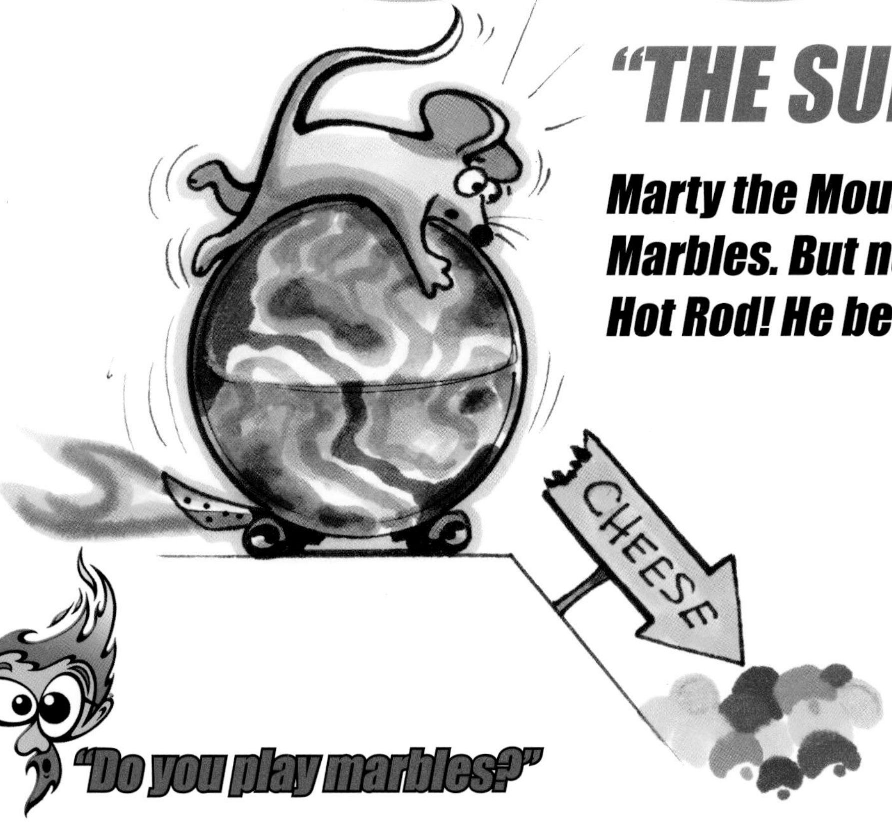
CHEESE

"THE SUPER ROLLER!"

Marty the Mouse loves to play Marbles. But now he's got a Marble Hot Rod! He better hold on tight.

"Do you play marbles?"

"OVERHEAD SLAM!"

The pilot of this power ball knows speed and he even has a helmet to match!

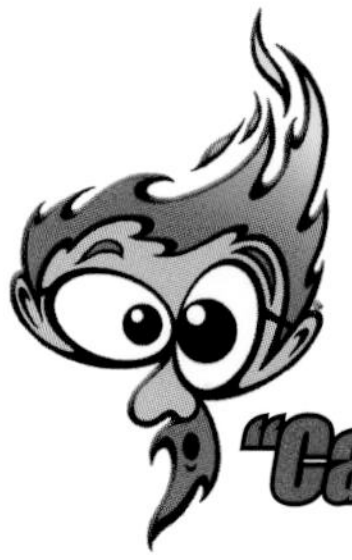

"Can you name what other sports use a ball?"

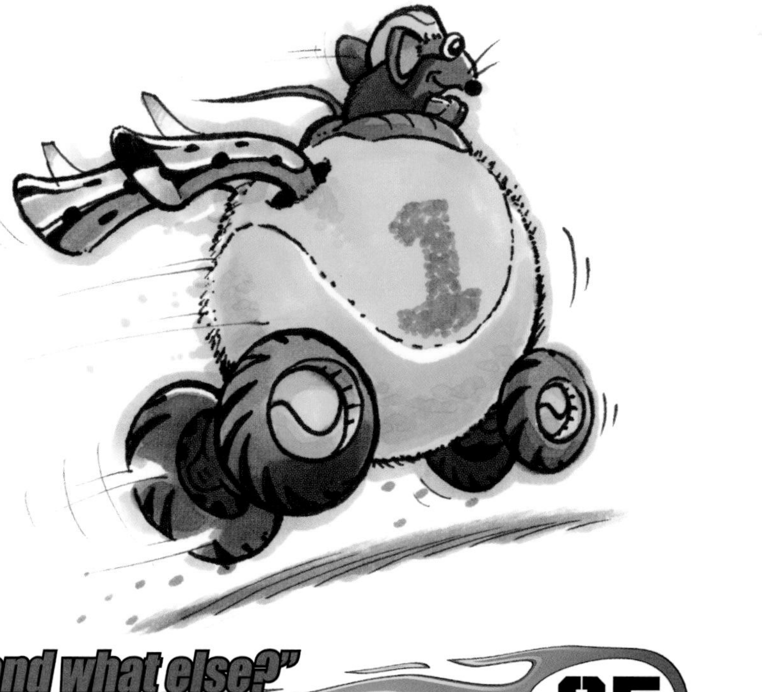

"SILVER KEYSTER!"

With this key, Mr. Morey Mouse can unlock his true speed. But just holding on is the key.

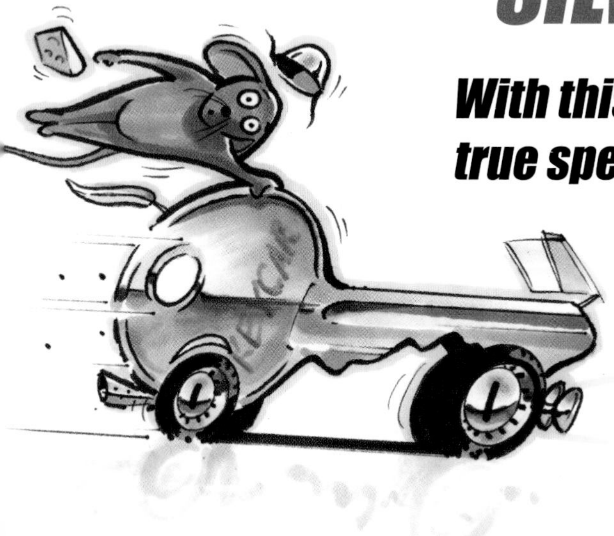

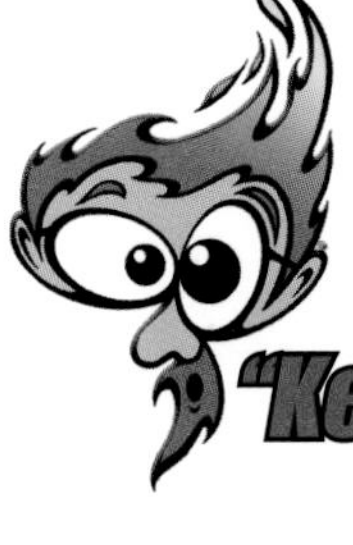

"Keys open doors, boxes, cars and what else?"

"GO, FISH, GO!"

Gorty and Gertrude the Goldfish love to go to the movies. And the Drive-In is their favorite.

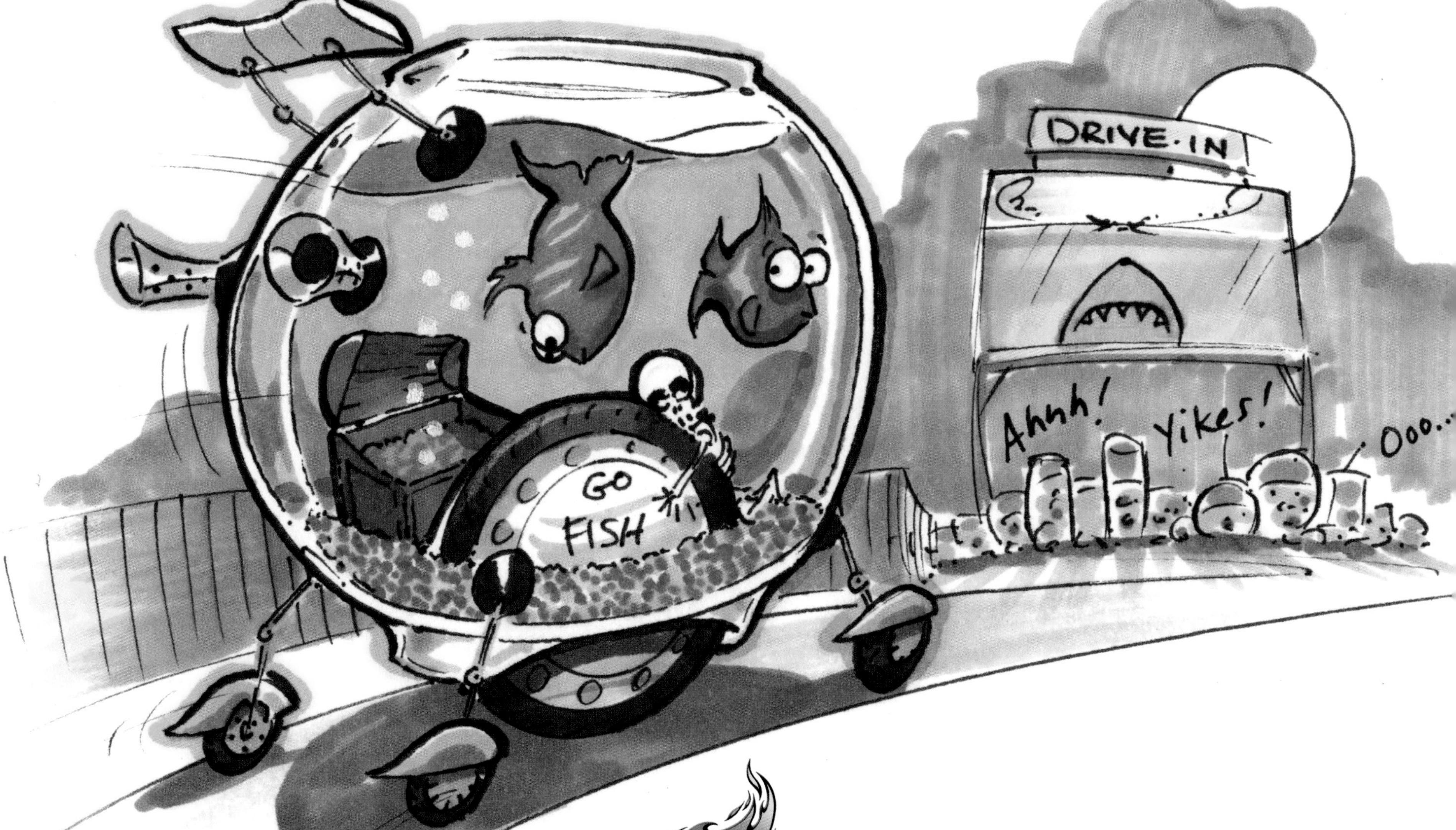
DRIVE-IN
GO FISH
Ahhh!
Yikes!
Ooo...

"Where's your favorite place to travel?"

TRAVELLERS

"BOOT RESCUE!"

This cool car is run by Sam, Sliver and Sally of "Off Trail Squirrel Rescue." And sometimes Morty the Mouse tags along. They'll go anywhere in the world to save their friends who may be in a jam.

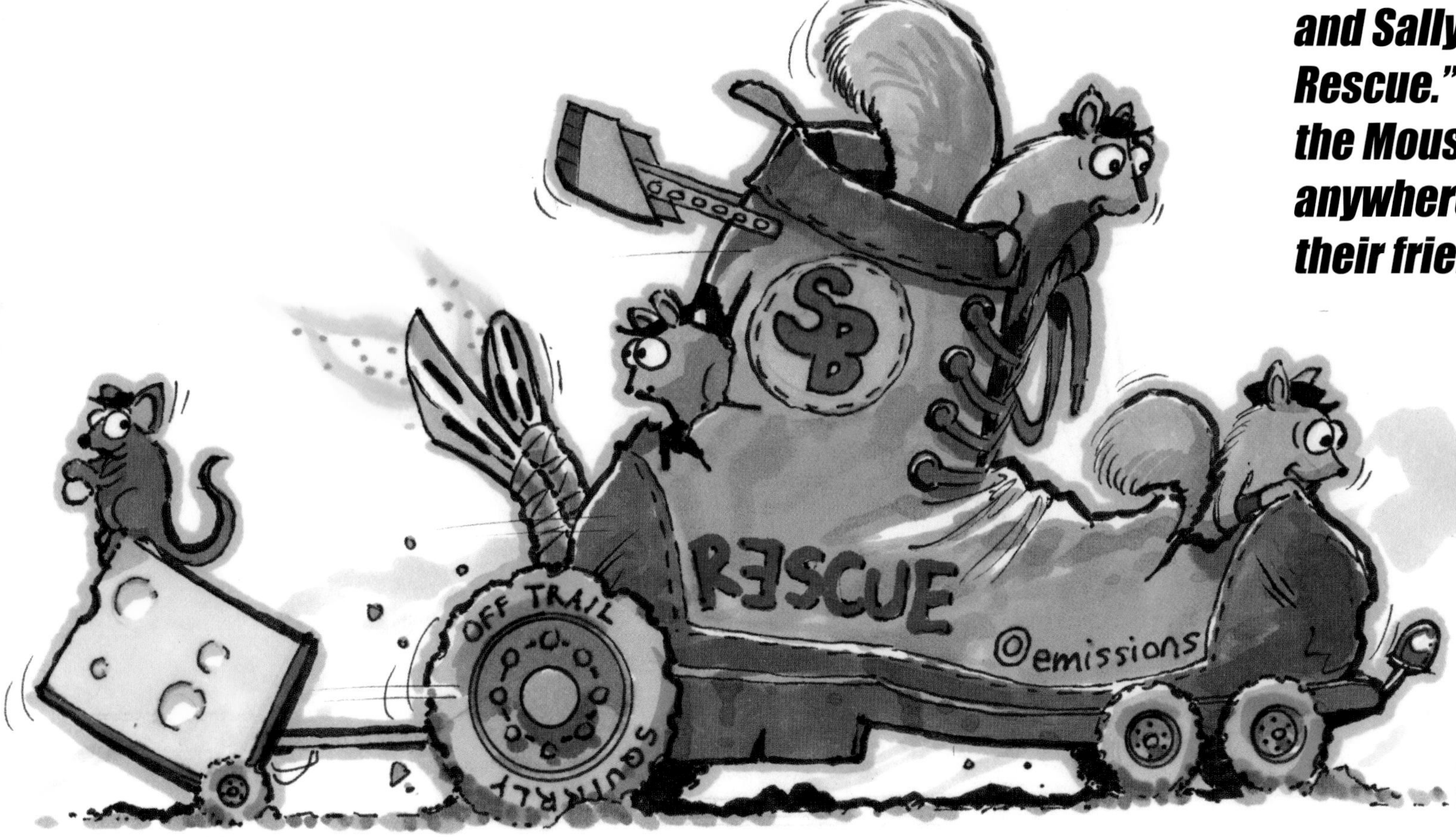

SB
RESCUE
OFF TRAIL
0 emissions

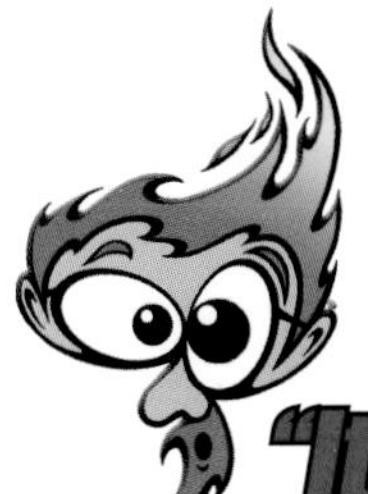

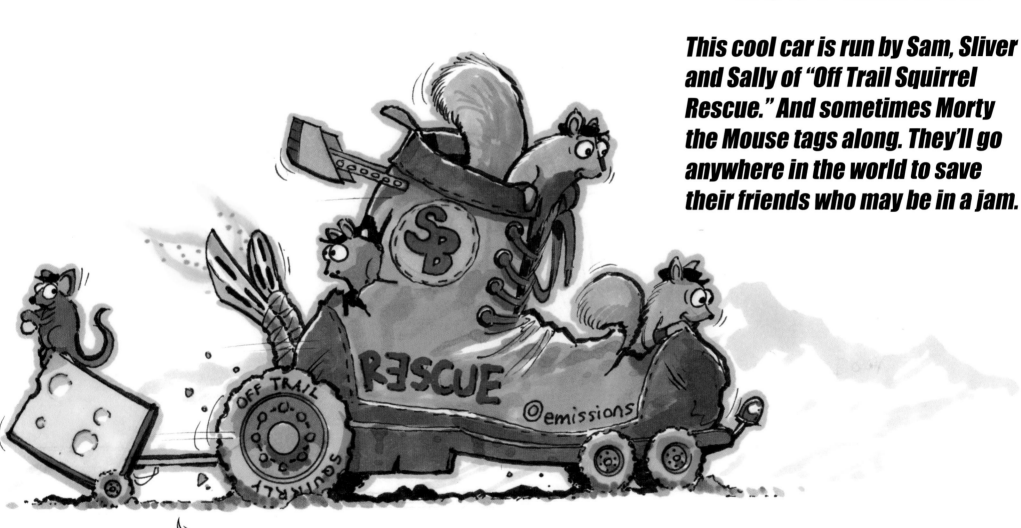

"It's always important to help your friends, right?"

"THE CARROT STICKSTER!"

Carrots are good for you, but they make cool cars, too!

"What other vegetables are good for you?"

STERS

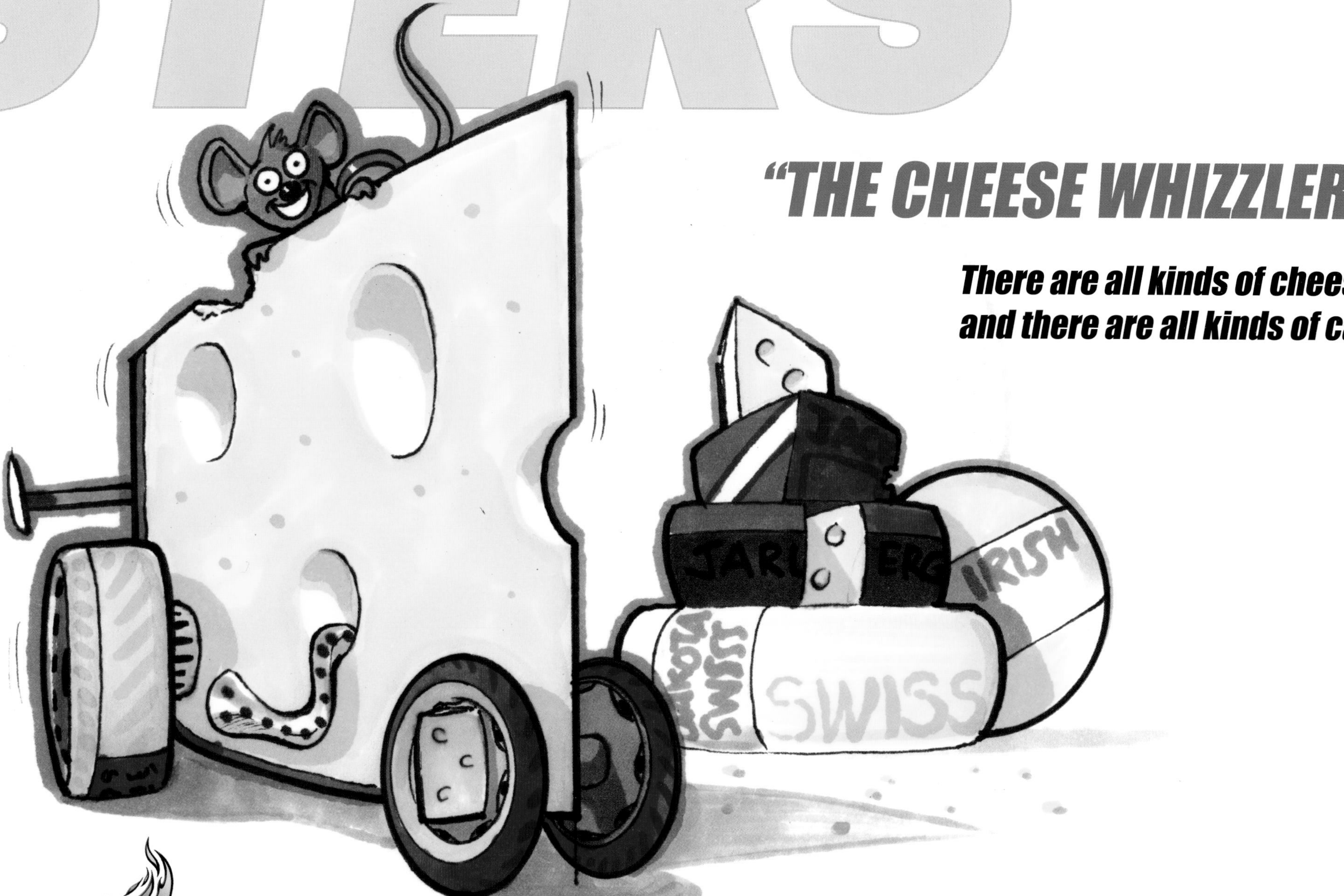
IRISH
SWISS

"THE CHEESE WHIZZLER!"

There are all kinds of cheeses, and there are all kinds of cars.

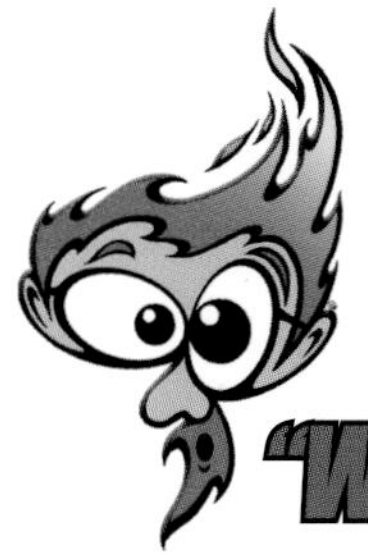

"What's your favorite cheese and what kind of car would it make?"

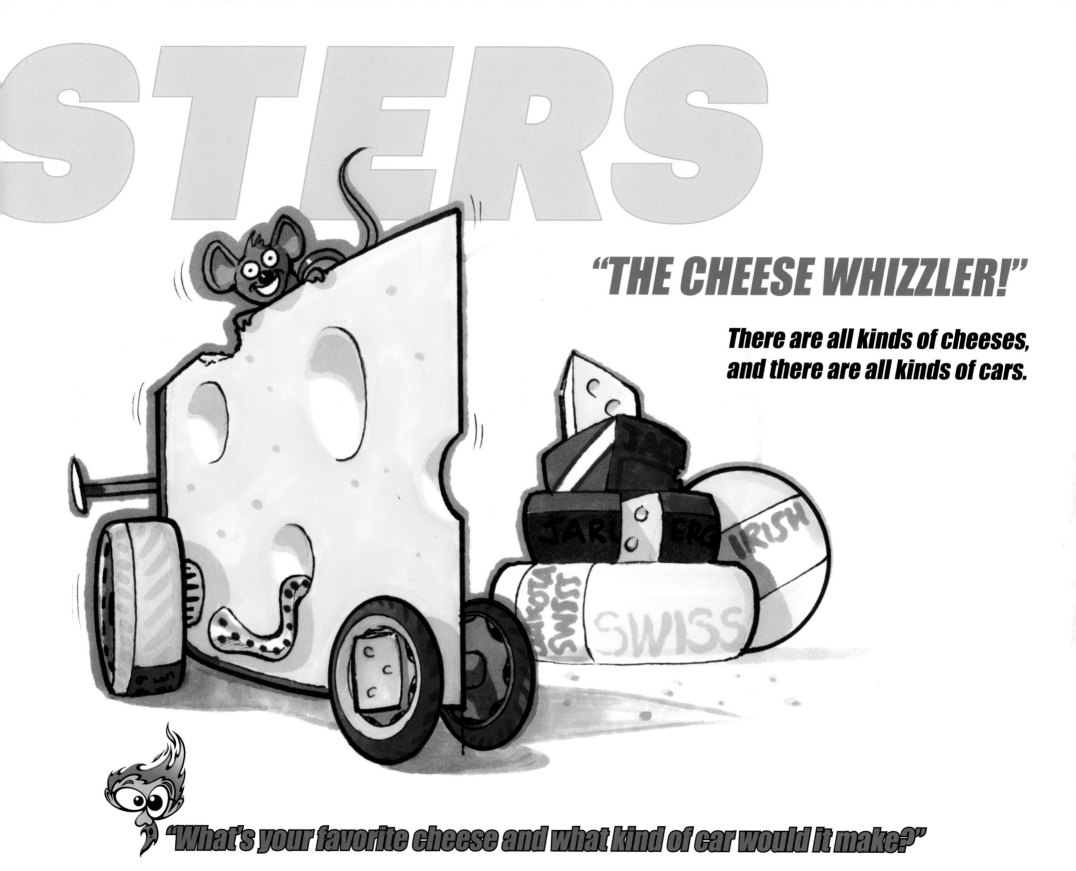

Yum

"THE GUMBALLER!"

This team of mice loves to shoot the gumball slide. And they can take this cool car wherever they go!

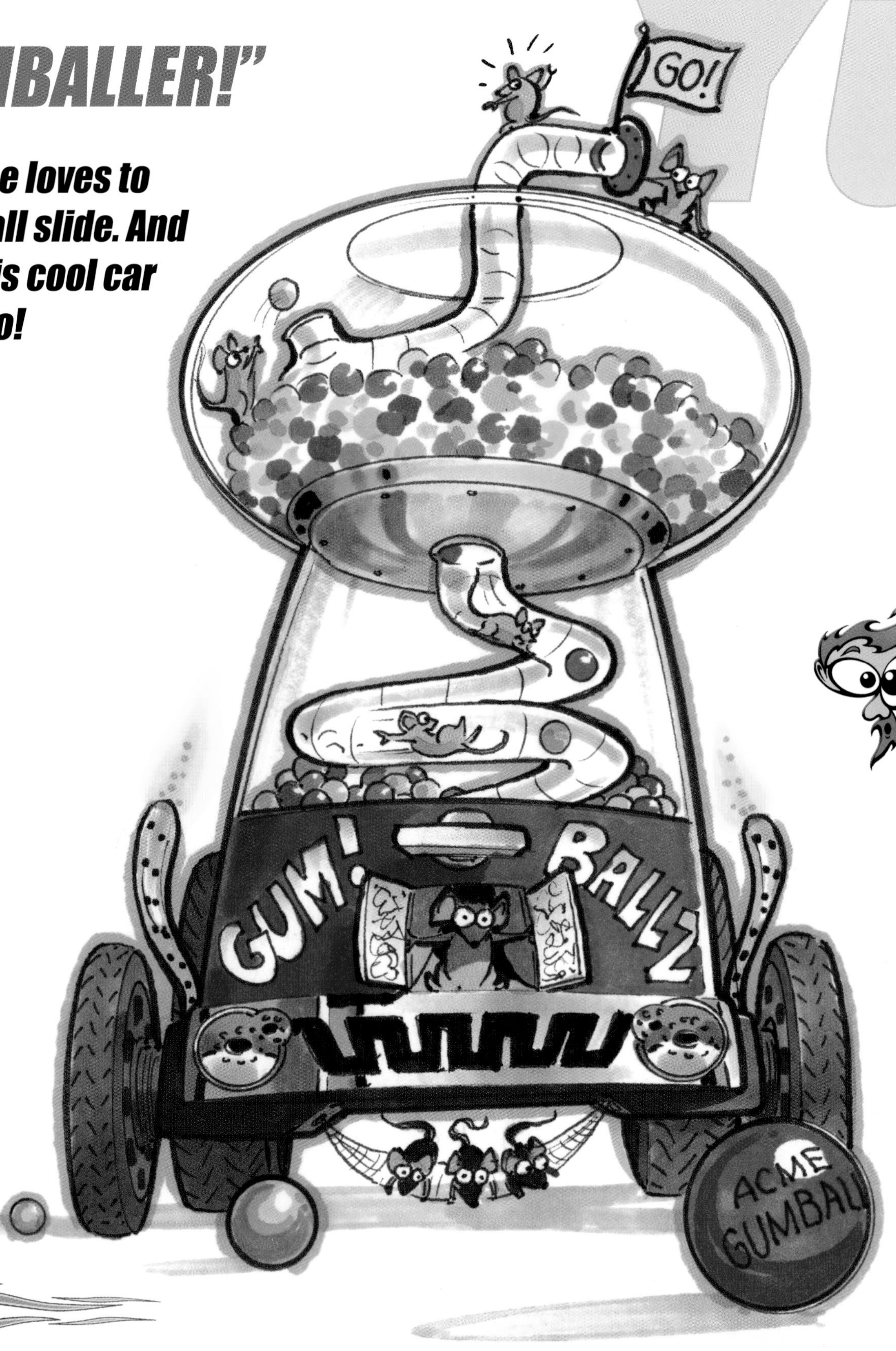
GO!
GUM!
BALLZ
ACME
GUMBALL

"Where do you go to have fun?"

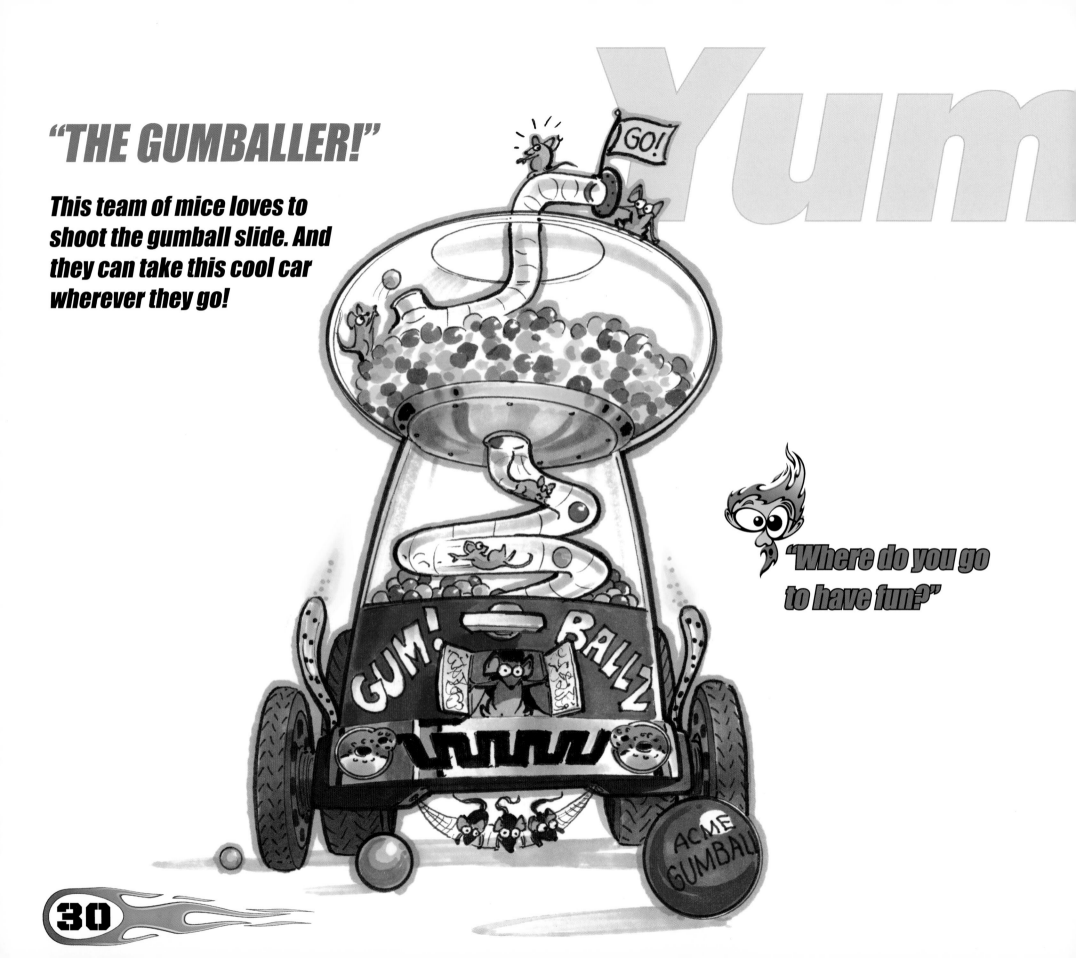

STERS

"PIZZA PEPPER POPPER!"

This bell pepper can really pop. And Miguel the mouse knows how to drive it. Especially to the pizza place!

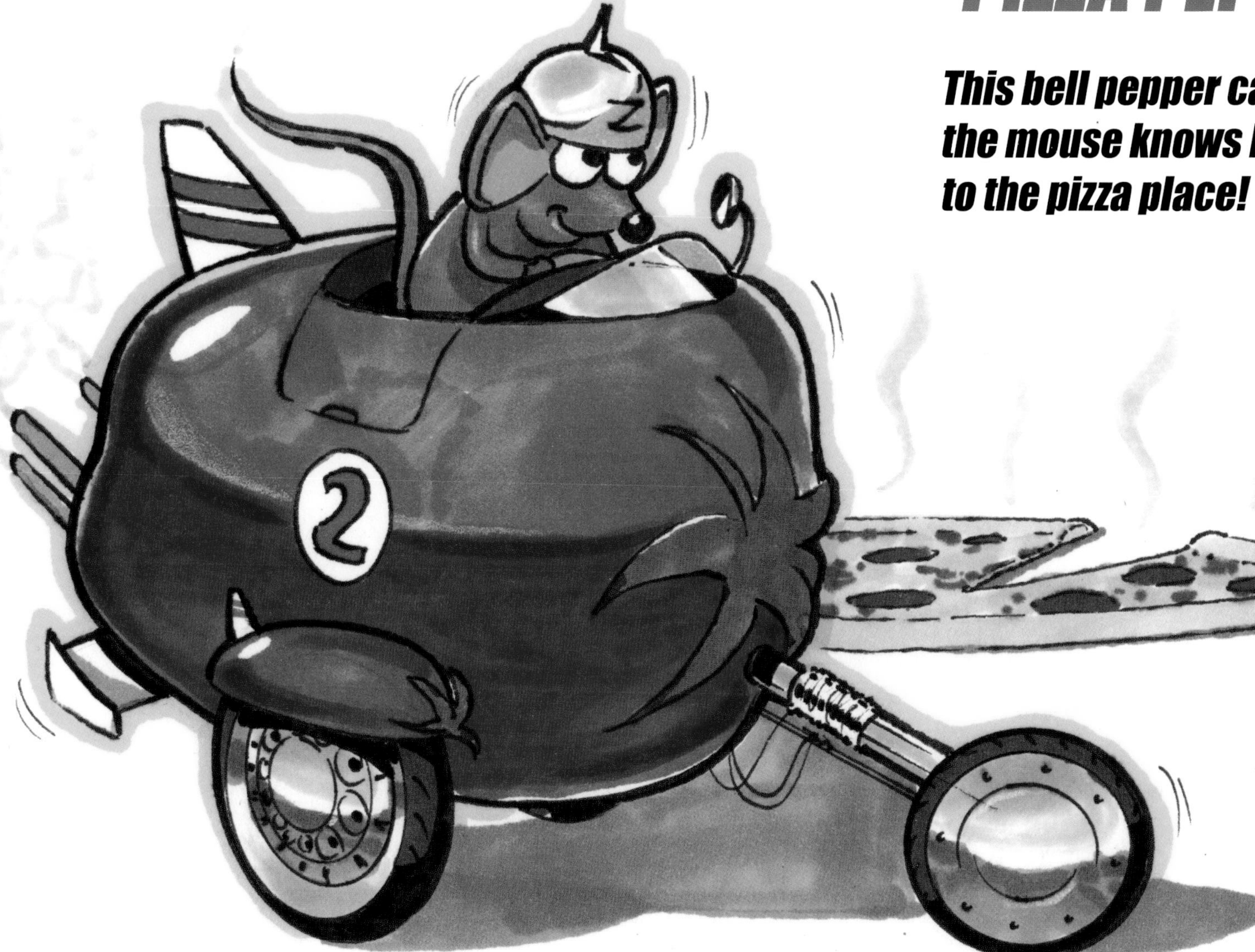

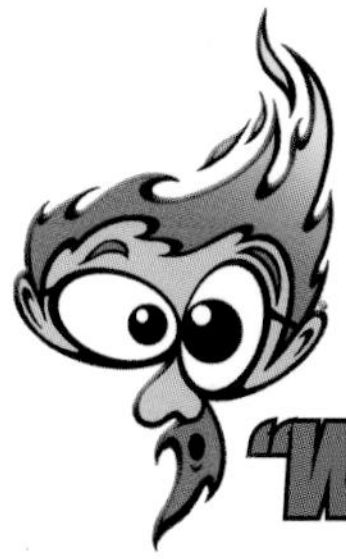
"What's your favorite food?"

Fireball Tim and Design Studio Press are proud to donate a portion of the proceeds from the sales of this book to Animal Care Programs.

Follow Fireball Tim online:

BLOG!

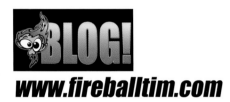

www.fireballtim.com

twitter

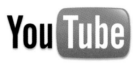

twitter.com/fireballtim

facebook

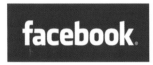

www.facebook.com/fireball.tim

YouTube

www.youtube.com/fireballtim

To order additional copies of this book and to view other books we offer, please visit:
www.designstudiopress.com

For volume purchases and resale inquiries, please email:
info@designstudiopress.com

Or you can write to:
Design Studio Press
8577 Higuera Street
Culver City, CA 90232

Telephone: 310.836.3116
Fax: 310.836.1136

To be notified of new releases, special discounts, and events, please sign up for our mailing list on our website, join our Facebook fan page, or follow us on Twitter:

www.facebook.com/designstudiopress

twitter.com/dstudiopress

Published by
Design Studio Press
8577 Higuera Street
Culver City, CA 90232

Website: www.designstudiopress.com
Email: info@designstudiopress.com

10 9 8 7 6 5 4 3 2 1

Printed in China
First edition, January 2013

Hardcover ISBN: 978-193349281-0
Library of Congress Control Number: 2012949082

designstudio PRESS

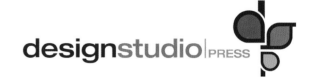